THE AMAZING tomato

PHOTOGRAPHY BY QUENTIN BACON

STYLING BY ANNE MARSHALL

BayBooks

An imprint of HarperCollins*Publishers*

STOCKISTS

Accoutrement
Shop 507 The Carousel
Bondi Junction NSW
Tel: (02) 387 8468

Appley Hoare Antiques
55 Queen Street
Woollahra NSW
Tel: (02) 362 3045

The Bay Tree
40 Holdsworth Street
Woollahra NSW
Tel: (02) 328 1101

Villa Italiana
566 Military Road
Mosman NSW
Tel: (02) 960 1788

A BAY BOOKS PUBLICATION

Bay Books, an imprint of
HarperCollins*Publishers*
25 Ryde Road, Pymble, Sydney NSW 2073, Australia
31 View Road, Glenfield, Auckland 10, New Zealand

First published in Australia in 1994

Copyright © Bay Books 1994

National Library of Australia
Cataloguing-in-Publication data:

The Amazing tomato cookbook.
  New ed.
    ISBN 1 86378 171 4.
    1. Cookery (Tomatoes). I. Marshall, Anne, 1938-
641.65642

Chapter openers and some internal photography: Quentin Bacon
Chapter openers and some internal food styling: Anne Marshall
Front cover food stylist: Donna Hay
Front cover home economist: Jody Vassallo
Front cover photography: Jon Bader
Front cover recipe: Mixed Tomato Tart

Printed by Griffin Press, Adelaide
Printed in Australia
9 8 7 6 5 4 3 2 1
96 95 94

CONTENTS

4

THE AMAZING TOMATO

10

SAUCES AND SALSAS

22

TOMATO SOUPS

30

PIZZAS AND PIES

46

SALADS AND JUICES

60

SNACKS AND FINGER FOOD

72

TOMATO CLASSICS

84

SUN-DRIED TOMATOES,
CHUTNEYS AND PRESERVES

94

MEASURING MADE EASY

95

INDEX

The Amazing Tomato

Tomatoes, with their glorious colour, tantalising aroma and distinctive flavour are truly amazing.

The *Lycopersicon esculentum*, or tomato, is botanically defined as a fruit but is generally used worldwide as a vegetable.

The tomato was first discovered by the Aztec Indians of South America and Mexico, growing like a weed in their maize (corn) crops. They called it a 'tomatl'.

The tomato was borne back to Europe from Mexico by the gold-seeking Spanish conquistadors, who prized the decorative qualities of the original yellow-coloured fruit.

When introduced to the Spanish-ruled kingdom of Naples, in Italy, it was christened 'pomo d'oro' or golden apple.

The visiting Moors called it 'pomi de mori' and when the tomato was introduced to France, the French translated the Moors' name to 'pomme d'amour' or 'love apple'! Amazing indeed!

The tomato is now ranked among the four most popular vegetables consumed in the Western world, along with the potato, onion and carrot. Thanks to a wide range of climates and modern transportation, tomatoes are now available all year round.

However, there is nothing to beat the flavour of a home-grown 'Grose Lise' tomato ripened on the vine. Due to consumer demand, the commercial tomato growers are now producing vine-ripened tomatoes which are much more flavoursome and better in texture than those which are picked before they have naturally ripened.

The sunny Mediterranean countries have naturally produced an abundance of popular tomato recipes. The gazpacho of Spain, the Provençale of France, the Napoletana of Italy and the stuffed tomatoes of Greece and Turkey are now international favourites. Adventurous cooks worldwide continue to develop more and more delicious tomato dishes with a spoonful of Mediterranean sunshine and flavour added to every one of them.

The versatility of the amazing tomato extends to processing too. It is available canned, puréed, in a robust-flavoured paste, in ketchup-style sauces and tasty pasta sauces, in chutneys and now sun-dried, sun-dried in oil and even as tomato pâté.

Nutritionally, tomatoes are a good source of vitamin C and a fair source of vitamin A, potassium and magnesium. They contain fibre, are low in kilojoules (calories) and are important in a healthy well-balanced diet.

WHAT TO LOOK FOR WHEN BUYING

SIZE This will depend on personal preference and on how the tomatoes are to be used. Studies

have shown that most people prefer a medium-sized, 6.5 cm to 7.5 cm (2½ in to 3 in) in diameter, tomato. This size is probably the most convenient to use in salads, sandwiches and as individual servings.

COLOUR Look for overall uniformity of colour in each fruit. Tomatoes continue to ripen after harvest, so the degree of colour required will depend on when the tomatoes are to be used. If you buy them only once a week, select a range of colours from pink to full red, remembering that, these days, even red tomatoes will keep much longer than previously. Include some pink and light red tomatoes for eating later in the week.

FIRMNESS People generally prefer firm tomatoes, especially for salads and sandwiches. Choose fruits that yield only slightly to moderate pressure from your hand, then only a few drops of juice or seeds will be lost when the tomato is sliced. With most present-day varieties even very red tomatoes will be firm.

BLEMISHES AND ROTS Rots are only a minor problem nowadays and any blemished fruits should be culled before they reach the shop. Do not select tomatoes that are bruised, split, grossly misshapen or have any obvious rot marks. Fruits showing uneven or blotchy yellow-orange areas may have been chilled or exposed to too high temperatures. They will have poor flavour, will not ripen properly and may develop rots.

STORING TOMATOES

Tomatoes should not be stored in the refrigerator for more than 4 days; the temperature, even in the crisper, is too low. Although tomatoes will obviously require different handling at different times of the year, the following points should be kept in mind:

- The best temperature for ripening tomatoes is 20°C (68°F), so store fruits that retain any green colour in a cupboard or on the bench away from direct sunlight, where they should ripen to a good flavour and texture. They do not need to be stored in the dark, but if they are exposed to direct sunlight they may become too hot and not ripen to the best flavour.
- In summer, fully red tomatoes can be stored for up to 4 days in the refrigerator crisper. But remember, they will gradually lose flavour and become sour and some soft or watery areas may develop in the flesh. For maximum flavour, remove them from the fridge at least one hour before eating.
- The best temperature for long storage of mature green fruits is

11°C to 12°C (51°F to 53°F) — warmer than the refrigerator and cooler than in most kitchens.

CAUSES OF POOR QUALITY

Problems with tomato quality have arisen because people in the marketing chain, including consumers, do not know how to handle the varieties that are now grown. Poor tomato quality has two main causes: either the tomatoes have been picked when they are still at the immature green stage or before they are fully grown, or they have ripened at temperatures that are too low or too high.

By following the above guidelines for quality selection and handling in the home, you should achieve greater satisfaction with this popular fruit.

The Publisher, Bay Books, wishes to thank and acknowledge the Department of Agriculture, New South Wales, for the above information on buying and storing tomatoes and on the causes of poor quality in tomatoes, taken from Agfacts, A Guide to Tomato Quality.

HEIRLOOM TOMATOES

Since its introduction to European agriculture, the tomato has been progressively cross-bred and changed. While tomatoes thrived in the sunny Mediterranean climate, much of their development has been directed towards producing forms which could be grown in areas with only short frost-free periods. Marmande or French Beefsteaks were the early successful cold-tolerant types and are the progenitors of several modern forms. Fashion subsequently dictated the colour and appearance of developing tomato strains. The bright red, round, smooth fruit we see today would be unrecognisable to the original importers of cultivated tomatoes.

Mass merchandising, cheap long-range transport and the growth of supermarkets have been the main determinants in tomato breeding in the last part of this century. Some attention has been given to appearance and colour but more emphasis has been placed on the ability of the fruit to withstand machine harvesting, rough packing and long-distance travel. The ultimate test for retailers is the ability of the tomato to be dropped from head height without breaking open. The resulting modern tomatoes are perfectly shaped but tough-skinned, and many consumers consider them tasteless. Recently there has been a resurgence of interest in old fashioned heirloom varieties. These are varieties that are no longer commercially available, but they have been saved and propagated by families or communities who preferred to keep growing them. At the moment, they are only available if you purchase seed and grow your own tomatoes, but the effects of consumer pressure on the suppliers of our fresh food has led to the presence of some flavourful vine ripened tomatoes in our shops again.

Description

The tomato (*Lycopersicon esculentum*) is a tender annual and requires at least a three month frost-free growing period to produce fruit. Tomatoes grow in two different ways, according to their variety.

'Determinate' or 'bush' tomatoes have shoots which are terminated by a flower cluster. New growth sprouts from below the flower cluster and is itself topped by a flower cluster. The resulting plant is compact, has many branches and generally requires minimal support.

'Indeterminate' or 'vining' tomatoes have a main shoot which will grow unchecked, bearing flower clusters on side growths. New shoots or laterals grow from the leaf axils at the base of leaves and they also bear flower clusters. Vigorous varieties can end up as very large plants with multiple shoots which require training and support.

Variety

A fascinating range of tomato varieties is available for growing in the home garden, most of which are never seen in your local greengrocer's shop. Varieties can be selected for their use in cooking, for appearance on the plate or for reasons of taste. Yellow, white and green varieties, often referred to as 'low acid' types, appear to be less acidic because sweet flavours balance the strong tomato flavours that some people dislike and refer to as 'acid'.

The most common tomatoes available now are beefsteaks, which are excellent slicing tomatoes and particularly attractive if sliced horizontally so that the regular pattern of flesh and seeds can be seen. Nothing could be tastier than a slice of a freshly harvested beefsteak tomato on a thick, crusty slice of sourdough bread, served with a drizzle of olive oil and a sprig of basil. Beefsteaks come in a wide range of sizes and colours. Reds range in size from the 200 g Rouge de Marmande to the 1.5 kg (3 lb) Mortgage Lifter. Colossal Yellow is a large tasty variety, White Beauty is similarly sized but has creamy, almost white, flesh and Greenwich is a green tomato when fully ripe. A slice of each of these varieties would form an attractive kaleidoscope of colours on a plate. For even further variety, a deep purple variety called Black can be grown.

Salad tomatoes are a little smaller than beefsteak types, generally not as juicy and hold their shape well when quartered. The size is about that of an apricot or plum and, like the beefsteaks, they come in a rainbow of colours. They are perfect for packed lunches or tossed into salads. The Red Peach variety is so named because the delicious pink fruits have a velvety appearance like that of a peach. Sunshine Girl is yellow, and Green Zebra is an apricot-sized green tomato with attractive yellow streaks. The red varieties Tommy Toe and Peruvian Sugarlump are probably the most prolific types of all, and two bushes will provide more fruit than a normal family can eat.

Italian culinary methods led to the development of paste or Roma tomatoes. These are oval in shape with a relatively thick skin and a high ratio of flesh to seed pulp which means thick sauces can be made with the minimum of boiling to reduce liquid. The seeds separate from the wall of the fruit which makes de-seeding very easy, and the shape makes for easy bottling and canning. Varieties available include San Marzano, Lampadina Marzano, Napoli Paste and Roma Improved.

Roma tomatoes can be used for drying, but there are special varieties developed for this purpose, such as Principe Borghese, a bantam egg sized fruit. The flavour of Principe Borghese is rather bland at harvest but intensifies after drying. Once ripe, the fruit is held on the bush without rotting so the whole plant can be pulled up and hung upside down to dry. Normally, tomatoes are dried by slicing ripe fruit longitudinally and laying them out to dry in full sun, covering them with gauze if necessary to protect them from bird or insect attacks. Late in the season, when the sun has lost its strength, late crops of fruits can be dried in an oven (see recipes on page 88).

Stuffing tomatoes have firm, thick-fleshed walls around a large open cavity with few seeds. The top can be sliced off and the cavity filled with a filling such as low fat cottage cheese and chopped chives or basil. The shell is not as firm as a capsicum's, so only light baking or grilling can be tolerated.

Green Zebra

Tommy Toe

Principe Borghese, drying tomato

Mortgage Lifter

Yellow Verna

Brandy Wine

Varieties which can be used for stuffing include Shimmeig Stoo (red with yellow stripes), Green Bell Pepper (green), and the Italian heirloom Costoluto Genovest which is also perfect for pastes.

Oxheart-type tomatoes are well known for their excellent flavours but are also ideal for preserving and bottling. The flesh is meaty and sweet with very few seeds and it boils down to pulp easily. The most productive types are Oxheart (rosy pink), Verna Orange (orange fleshed), Sherry's Sweet Italian (red, cone shaped) and the multiple-purpose heirloom Amish Paste.

Tomatoes smaller than a coin are known as cherry tomatoes and are generally available in shops. They are very early, prolific and ideal for cultivation in pots.

The flavour of smaller tomatoes tends to be the most intense of all and they can be used to great effect in small side salads, for garnishing entrées or as a more unusual crudité. Popular varieties are Tiny Tim, Sweet 100 or the sweet yellow variety Broad Ripple Yellow Currant.

Cultivation

Full sun, well-drained soil and temperatures above 15°C are the recipe for successful tomato growing.

Tomato seed should be sown indoors in punnets or pots in a good quality seed-raising mixture. This should be carried out eight to ten weeks before you expect to plant them out into their final position. Germination should take seven to ten days, and when the seedlings have a couple of leaves, they should be planted into larger pots.

Established tomato plants can be bought from garden centres in punnets or in individual pots just before planting. Be sure to buy hardened-off seedlings, with dark green firm growth, not light green soft growth.

The position where you are going to plant the tomatoes should have been dug to a spade depth, weeded, and the soil clods broken up to a good tilth. It is best to incorporate some well-rotted animal manure while digging, then hill up the soil to form mounds to help with drainage. Plant the

tomato seedlings deeply into the mounds so that the first true leaves are level with the soil. The ideal spacing for tomatoes is 50 cm (20 in) apart, with 1 m (3¼ ft) between the rows. Tomato plants can grow very large when grown well, so closer spacing can be harder to manage.

In cool areas where frosts occur, such as southern Australia, tomatoes should not be planted before October or after December. In warmer frost-free areas, plants can be set out from August onwards, and in subtropical areas they can be grown all year round.

Tomato plants naturally regulate fruit set and drop their excess fruit, so pruning is only really needed to control growth and allow the easy picking of fruit. Most bush types will need little pruning, but stems which are out of place can be removed. Vining tomato types are best pruned to a number of main shoots, followed by removal of the new lateral growths to keep them manageable, but if too much foliage is removed the fruit can get sunburnt. Shoots should be tied to supports because the weight of developing fruit will cause the plants to collapse. The kind of support provided will determine the number of main shoots to leaves.

Animal manures or a complete fertiliser low in nitrogen should be applied at planting. A side dressing of fowl manure or nitrogenous fertilisers at first fruit set, followed by fortnightly foliar feeds with organic liquid fertilisers, will improve the quality and quantity of the crop.

Watering is of critical importance for the production of good quality tomatoes. While the seedlings are young, care should be taken not to over-water them. Once the first fruit is set, the water requirements are greater and in warm weather the equivalent of 25 mm (1 in) of rain every three days is needed. Water should be applied around the roots and not over the foliage, and is best done regularly to avoid putting the plants under stress, which would leave them susceptible to problems such as blossom end rot.

The fruit can be harvested when it starts to change colour, then allowed to ripen fully indoors. In the case of red tomatoes, the colouring becomes a pink blush. Other coloured tomatoes show other changes of colour. The fruit can be allowed to ripen completely on the vine, but birds will often damage the fruit and soft rots (botrytis) can also attack the fruit. For late tomatoes, whole branches with unripe fruit on them can be harvested before the first frosts and stored in a warm place to ripen.

Problems

Tomatoes can be affected by a number of disorders but most can be solved by good cultural practices.

Soil-borne problems such as nematodes, sclerotina and verticillium and fusarium wilts can be minimised by planting in freshly cultivated ground not used for tomatoes, capsicums, aubergines or potatoes in the last year. Any diseased plants should be burned and not composted.

Mulching with compost or straw helps control weeds and stops the soil drying out too quickly. It also helps minimise the water splash spread of soil-borne diseases and alternaria leaf spot.

Caterpillars can be easily controlled by removal when inspecting the plants. Thrips and leaf hoppers may need to be sprayed because they spread such diseases as spotted wilt virus and big bud mycoplasma.

Poor fruit set usually occurs because the temperature is not suitable. Early in the season, low night temperatures result in poor pollination, which improves when temperatures rise above 15°C (60°F). For early fruit, grow early-bearing varieties which can set fruit at lower temperatures. High temperatures (above 38°C/100°F) can cause flower and young fruit drop and the effects of a hot spell can be seen for many days afterwards. Some varieties, such as Tropic, are more tolerant of hot weather.

Sources

Seed and seedlings of standard tomato varieties can be obtained at most garden centres and nurseries. The more unusual types are obtainable from the mail order suppliers listed below:

- BROERSEN SEEDS AND BULBS
  365 Monbulk Road, Monbulk, Vic 3795.
- DIGGER'S SEEDS
  105 Latrobe Parade, Dromana, Vic 3936.
- EDEN SEEDS
  MS 316, Gympie, Qld 4570.
- NEW GIPPSLAND SEED FARM
  PO Box 1, Silvan, Vic 3795.
- PHOENIX SEEDS
  PO Box 207, Snugg, Tas 7054.

Pictures of Heirloom tomato varieties and text on the history and growing of tomatoes suppled by Will Ashburner of Digger's Club.

Sauces and Salsas

*T*omato sauces turn pasta into a memorable meal. Tangy tomato salsas, hot and cold, are delicious with fish. Spicy curry tomato sauces can be taste temptations with vegetables, prawns and barbecues. Anything and everything goes with tomato sauces and salsas!

Mould the potato mixture into walnut-sized balls, using lightly floured fingers.

Poach Potato Gnocchi in boiling salted water.

Pictured on previous pages: Penne with Tomato and Olive Sauce (page 20), Fresh Tomato Salsa (page 16)

GNOCCHI WITH RIPE TOMATO SAUCE

5 medium-sized potatoes, peeled and chopped

150 g (5 oz) plain flour

2 eggs, beaten

SAUCE

5 large ripe tomatoes, peeled, cored and chopped

1 tablespoon tomato paste

3 tablespoons sliced sun-dried tomatoes

salt and pepper

60 g (2 oz) butter

grated Parmesan cheese and chopped parsley, to garnish

Boil the potatoes until tender, then drain and mash. Fold in the flour and eggs, then set the mixture aside to cool slightly.

To Prepare Sauce: Put the tomatoes, tomato paste, sun-dried tomatoes, salt, pepper and butter into a shallow pan and bring to the boil. Reduce the heat and simmer for 15 to 20 minutes until a thick consistency. Set aside until required.

Form the potato dough into small walnut-sized balls. Preheat oven to 200°C (400°F).

Bring a large pan of salted water to the boil, drop 4 to 6 gnocchi into the water and cook at simmering point for 10 to 12 minutes or until the gnocchi float to the surface. Remove with a slotted spoon and drain. Continue in this way until all the gnocchi are cooked. Divide the gnocchi into 4 to 6 individual oven-proof dishes. Spoon the tomato sauce over the gnocchi, then sprinkle with Parmesan cheese. Bake for 10 to 15 minutes or until bubbling and brown. Sprinkle with parsley and serve, accompanied by a crisp green salad.

SERVES 4 TO 6

BASIL

Basil is one of the most popular herbs. It has a rich spicy flavour. Fresh basil leaves can be stored for a few days in plastic bags in the refrigerator or blanched in boiling water and frozen.

PASTA WITH SUN-DRIED TOMATO PESTO

400 g (13 oz) vegetable pasta

SAUCE

½ cup sun-dried tomatoes, in oil, drained

6 cherry tomatoes, halved

2 cloves garlic, crushed

3 tablespoons pine nuts

1 cup fresh basil leaves or continental parsley

3 tablespoons olive oil

60 g (2 oz) grated Parmesan cheese

extra grated Parmesan cheese, to garnish

Cook pasta in a large pan of boiling salted water until al dente.

To Prepare Sauce: Place sun-dried tomatoes, cherry tomatoes, garlic, pine nuts and basil in a food processor and mix well. Stop and scrape down the sides of the food processor, add oil and mix again. Stir Parmesan cheese into the sauce.

Serve freshly cooked hot pasta in individual pasta bowls and spoon sauce over, allowing it to run through the pasta.

Serve immediately, sprinkled with extra grated Parmesan cheese, accompanied by a green salad.

SERVES 4

Pasta with Sun-dried Tomato Pesto

CAULIFLOWER KOFTAS IN HOT TOMATO SAUCE

HOT TOMATO SAUCE

12 large, ripe tomatoes

1 tablespoon brown sugar

1 bay leaf

½ teaspoon salt

1 tablespoon paprika

30 g (1 oz) butter or margarine

1 tablespoon chopped fresh basil or mint

KOFTAS

1 large cauliflower

90 g (3 oz) chick pea flour (also called 'besan' flour)

1 teaspoon ground cumin

1 teaspoon ground coriander

1 teaspoon ground turmeric

¼ teaspoon ground ginger

½ teaspoon ground fenugreek

2 teaspoons salt

¼ teaspoon cayenne pepper

1 egg, lightly beaten

ghee, for deep frying

To Prepare Hot Tomato Sauce: Remove cores from tomatoes, cut into wedges and mix to a purée in a food processor or blender. Pour the tomato purée into a saucepan and bring to the boil. Add brown sugar, bay leaf, salt, paprika, butter and basil then simmer uncovered, until the mixture thickens. Keep warm until required.

To Prepare Koftas: Grate cauliflower finely, then add the chick pea flour, all the spices, salt, cayenne pepper and egg. Mix well. Heat ghee in a deep fryer. Squeeze the cauliflower mixture into walnut-sized balls, then fry small batches in the hot ghee until firm and dark brown. Remove from the ghee, drain on paper towels and arrange on a serving plate.

Pour the hot tomato sauce over the koftas, allowing them to soak in it for a few minutes before serving. Serve as part of an Indian meal.

Note: Do not grate the cauliflower until ready to use because it becomes very moist.

SERVES 6 TO 8

PASTA WITH TOMATO AND MUSHROOM SAUCE

30 g (1 oz) butter or margarine

8 shallots (spring onions), chopped

125 g (4 oz) mushrooms, chopped

2 large ripe tomatoes, cored and chopped

¼ cup (60 ml/2 fl oz) light sour cream

400 g to 500 g (13 oz to 16 oz) spaghetti or rigatoni

grated Parmesan cheese, to garnish

Melt butter in a saucepan and gently fry shallots (spring onions) and mushrooms. Add tomatoes and simmer for 10 minutes or until the mixture thickens. Add the sour cream and cook for 1 minute more.

Pour sauce over freshly cooked pasta, sprinkle with Parmesan cheese and serve, accompanied by a green salad.

SERVES 4

Cauliflower Koftas in Hot Tomato Sauce

TOMATO BARBECUE SAUCE

30 g (1 oz) butter or margarine

1 large onion, finely chopped

2 tablespoons brown sugar

1 tablespoon malt vinegar

1 tablespoon Worcestershire or soy sauce

1 cup peeled, seeded, finely chopped tomatoes

2 tablespoons tomato paste

2 tablespoons lemon juice

Heat butter in a saucepan and gently fry onion until soft and golden. Add all remaining ingredients. Bring to the boil, then simmer for 15 minutes.

Serve sauce warm or cold with barbecued steak, chops, sausages or burgers.

SERVES 8

TOMATO SEAFOOD SAUCE WITH OYSTER AND CALAMARI FRITTERS

TOMATO SEAFOOD SAUCE

1 cup (250 ml/8 fl oz) mayonnaise

1 tablespoon sweet chilli sauce

2 tablespoons tomato paste

salt and pepper

1 tablespoon chopped chives

4 shallots (spring onions), thinly sliced

1 teaspoon chopped capers

BATTER

60 g (2 oz) plain flour

pinch salt

⅓ cup (80 ml/4 fl oz) warm water

1 tablespoon olive oil

1 tablespoon chopped fresh parsley

1 egg, stiffly whisked

FRITTERS

20 to 30 oysters

16 to 24 calamari rings

oil, for deep frying

lemon wedges and parsley, to garnish

To Prepare Tomato Seafood Sauce: Combine all the sauce ingredients. Chill until ready for use.

To Prepare Batter: Sieve flour and salt into a bowl, then mix in the water, oil and parsley. Fold in the egg white.

To Prepare Fritters: Drain oysters and calamari on paper towels. To finish fritters, dip each oyster and calamari ring into the batter until coated and deep fry, a few at a time, until crisp and golden. Drain on paper towels.

Serve the fritters hot with the Tomato Seafood Sauce and garnish with lemon wedges and parsley.

SERVES 4 TO 6

CALAMARI

Calamari can be purchased whole, in tubes or in rings. The way you purchase it will depend on how much preparation you wish to do. If you buy it whole, simply remove the head and tentacles from the hood. Remove skin and flaps from hood by pulling firmly. Rinse under cold water.

Slice into rings.

NAPOLITANA SAUCE

A very versatile sauce which is used in many delicious tomato dishes.

1 tablespoon olive oil

2 onions, chopped

2 cloves garlic, crushed

5 ripe tomatoes, cored and coarsely chopped

2 tablespoons tomato paste

1 tablespoon chopped fresh oregano or 1 teaspoon dried oregano

1 tablespoon chopped fresh basil or 1 teaspoon dried basil

1 teaspoon sugar

salt and pepper

500 g (1 lb) pasta or 2 pizza bases

Heat oil in a pan and gently fry onions and garlic until golden brown. Add the remaining ingredients and simmer uncovered for 20 to 30 minutes or until thick. Adjust seasoning.

Serve sauce hot over freshly cooked pasta or spread over pizza bases when making savoury pizzas.

Canned tomatoes may be used in place of fresh tomatoes for convenience. The resulting sauce is colourful and flavoursome.

SERVES 4 OR MAKES 2 PIZZAS

FRESH TOMATO SALSA

Pictured on pages 10-11.

This fresh spicy tomato sauce is delicious with prawns (shrimps), crab salad or grilled fish. It is also low in kilojoules (calories), so it is good for a weight reduction diet. Delicious on top of scrambled eggs for brunch.

> *2 cups peeled, seeded, diced vine-ripened tomatoes*
>
> *1 small red Spanish onion, finely chopped*
>
> *1 red chilli pepper, seeded and finely chopped*
>
> *1 tablespoon sweet chilli sauce*
>
> *1 teaspoon balsamic vinegar*
>
> *1 tablespoon shredded fresh basil*
>
> *salt*

Mix all ingredients together, cover and chill in refrigerator for at least 30 minutes to allow flavours to blend and mature. Serve salsa with shellfish, grilled salmon or tuna, grilled whiting or trout or scrambled eggs.

Variation: Add 1 peeled and diced peach or nectarine when in season.

SERVES 8 TO 10

HOT TOMATO SALSA WITH STUFFED SQUID

HOT TOMATO SALSA

> *1 tablespoon olive oil*
>
> *2 French shallots, chopped*
>
> *425 g (13½ oz) can tomatoes, mashed*
>
> *1 tablespoon chopped fresh oregano*
>
> *salt and pepper*
>
> *2 red chillies, seeded and finely chopped*

STUFFED SQUID

> *8 to 12 medium to large size squid hoods*
>
> *4 anchovies, mashed*
>
> *1 clove garlic, crushed*
>
> *90 g (3 oz) fresh breadcrumbs*
>
> *2 tablespoons chopped fresh parsley*
>
> *1 egg, beaten*
>
> *freshly ground black pepper*
>
> *3 tablespoons olive oil*

To Prepare Hot Tomato Salsa: Heat oil in a heavy-based pan and gently fry shallots until soft. Add all remaining ingredients and bring to the boil.

To Prepare Stuffed Squid: Select squid that is cleaned and skinned, eliminating the messy job of cleaning the squid. Rinse the squid and dry it well. Mix anchovies, garlic, breadcrumbs, 1 tablespoon parsley, egg and pepper together, then fill the squid hoods with the anchovy mixture. Secure each opening with a toothpick.

Heat olive oil in a large frying pan, then add the squid. Cook until brown, then turn and brown the other side.

Transfer carefully to the salsa sauce, cover and simmer for 20 minutes or until tender.

Place 2 squid onto each entrée plate, spoon over the hot salsa tomato sauce and serve sprinkled with the rest of the parsley.

SERVES 4 TO 6

FISHERMAN'S BASKET WITH WINE TOMATO SALSA

> *300 g (10 oz) green prawns, shelled and deveined*
>
> *125 g (4 oz) crabmeat*
>
> *125 g (4 oz) thick fish fillet*
>
> *125 g (4 oz) scallops*
>
> *plain flour, seasoned with salt and pepper*
>
> *2 tablespoons vegetable oil*
>
> *1 clove garlic, chopped*
>
> *500 g (1 lb) ripe tomatoes, cored, peeled and chopped*
>
> *1 tablespoon balsamic vinegar*
>
> *2 tablespoons dry white wine*
>
> *salt and pepper*
>
> *2 tablespoons chopped fresh parsley*
>
> *2 tablespoons snipped chives*

Cut seafood, if necessary, into 2.5 cm (1 in) lengths. Coat all the seafood in the seasoned flour, shaking off any excess. Heat oil in a frying pan, then add the seafood. Fry until a light golden colour, turning frequently, then drain the seafood on paper towels. Keep hot.

Add garlic to pan and fry gently for 1 minute. Stir in the tomatoes and cook for 10 minutes more. Add the vinegar and wine and simmer until thickened. Season with salt and pepper. Add the parsley and chives.

Serve Wine Tomato Salsa with the hot fried seafood, accompanied by a green salad.

SERVES 4

SWEET AND SOUR TOMATO SAUCE WITH VEGETABLES

SWEET AND SOUR TOMATO SAUCE

- 10 large, ripe tomatoes, cored and chopped
- ¼ cup (60 ml/2 fl oz) apple cider vinegar
- 60 g (2 oz) brown sugar
- 4 tablespoons peanut oil
- 1 clove garlic, crushed
- 2 to 3 red chillies, chopped
- 1 teaspoon fenugreek seeds
- ¼ teaspoon anise seeds
- 1 teaspoon finely chopped ginger

VEGETABLES

- 1 red capsicum (pepper), cut into 2.5 cm (1 in) squares
- 1 green capsicum (pepper), cut into 2.5 cm (1 in) squares
- 3 carrots, cut into diagonal strips
- 2 stalks celery, cut into diagonal strips
- 1 small pineapple, cut into 2.5 cm (1 in) cubes
- ½ cup canned bamboo shoots, sliced
- ½ cup canned water chestnuts, sliced
- 125 g (4 oz) bean sprouts or shoots
- 125 g (4 oz) cashew nuts, roasted

To Prepare Sauce: Put tomatoes into a large pan and bring to the boil. Simmer uncovered, until tender. Stir the vinegar and brown sugar into the tomatoes.

Heat 1 tablespoon oil in a wok, add the garlic and chillies, and fry for 1 minute. Stir in the fenugreek, anise and ginger and stir-fry for 1 minute. Stir the spice mixture into the tomatoes.

To Prepare Vegetables: Heat remaining oil in wok and stir-fry the vegetables in the following order: red and green capsicum, carrot, celery, pineapple, bamboo shoots, water chestnuts and bean sprouts, until tender but still crisp. Add tomato sauce to the vegetables and simmer for a few minutes. Top with cashew nuts and serve with rice.

SERVES 6 TO 8

TOMATO AND CHICK PEA SUBJI

- 10 medium-sized tomatoes, cored and chopped
- 20 g (1 oz) ghee
- 1 teaspoon cumin seeds
- 4 to 6 small chillies, finely chopped
- 1 teaspoon ground coriander
- 1 teaspoon ground turmeric
- 2 teaspoons paprika
- 1 teaspoon salt
- 6 medium-sized zucchini (courgettes), cut into 2.5 cm (1 in) pieces
- 3 large capsicum (peppers), seeded and cut into 2.5 cm (1 in) pieces
- 400 g (13 oz) can chick peas (garbanzo beans), drained
- 2 teaspoons brown sugar
- 1 tablespoon shredded fresh basil or mint

Put tomatoes into a large pan, bring to the boil, then simmer uncovered until tender.

Heat ghee in a small pan, add cumin seeds and chillies and fry until brown. Stir in coriander and turmeric and cook until brown, then stir the spice mixture into the tomatoes. Season with paprika and salt.

Stir in the zucchini and capsicum, cover and simmer until soft. Add the chick peas, brown sugar and basil and simmer for a further 10 minutes, adding a little vegetable stock if more liquid is required.

Eat hot, sprinkled with fresh basil. Serve rice and curry accompaniments such as banana and yoghurt as side dishes.

SERVES 4 TO 6

TOFU WITH PEAS AND TOMATOES

- 8 large, ripe tomatoes, cored and peeled
- 250 g (8 oz) tofu
- juice of 1 lemon
- 2 tablespoons light soy sauce
- 20 g (1 oz) ghee
- 1 teaspoon cumin seeds
- 2 small chillies, chopped
- 1 teaspoon salt
- 1 tablespoon paprika
- 1 teaspoon ground coriander
- 1 tablespoon brown sugar
- 500 g (1 lb) shelled peas (or frozen peas, thawed)
- 2 tablespoons chopped fresh coriander, to garnish

Cut tomatoes into eight wedges and the tofu into 2.5 cm (1 in) cubes. Marinate tofu in lemon juice mixed with soy sauce. Heat ghee in a frying pan and fry the cumin seeds and chillies until brown, then add tomatoes, salt, paprika, coriander, brown sugar and peas. Cook covered, over medium heat for 10 minutes.

Add the tofu cubes and simmer for 5 minutes. Sprinkle with the fresh coriander and serve with brown or white rice.

SERVES 4

CURRIED TOMATO SAUCE WITH PRAWNS (SHRIMPS)

30 g (1 oz) butter or margarine

1 small onion, chopped

2 cloves garlic, crushed

1 tablespoon curry powder or paste

¼ teaspoon chilli powder

2 large tomatoes, cored and chopped

¾ cup (185 ml/6 fl oz) chicken stock

750 g (1½ lb) green prawns (shrimps), shelled and deveined

1 teaspoon lemon juice

2 hard-boiled eggs, quartered, to garnish

Melt butter in a heavy-based pan and gently fry onion and garlic until soft but not browned. Add the curry and chilli powders and stir over the heat for 1 minute. Add tomatoes and simmer over a low heat for 5 minutes, stirring frequently.

Pour in the stock, add prawns (shrimps) and simmer for 2 to 3 minutes, or until prawns (shrimps) are opaque and cooked. Mix in lemon juice. Simmer until heated through. Serve garnished with egg, accompanied by rice, pappadums and curry accompaniments such as banana and yoghurt.

SERVES 4

PROVENCALE SAUCE WITH GREEN BEANS

⅓ cup (80 ml/2½ fl oz) olive oil

2 onions, sliced

6 ripe tomatoes

3 cloves garlic, crushed

1 bouquet garni

salt and pepper

1 kg (2 lb) green beans, with ends trimmed

2 tablespoons chopped fresh parsley, to garnish

Heat oil in a large pan, add onions and cook over a gentle heat until soft (about 10 minutes).

Peel and core tomatoes. Remove and reserve the seeds and juices. Combine the seeds and juice with water to make 150 ml (5 fl oz) of liquid. Chop the tomato flesh. Add the tomatoes, garlic, bouquet garni and tomato liquid to the onions and season with salt and pepper. Bring to the boil, then reduce heat and simmer for 30 minutes.

Add beans to pan, cover and simmer for 10 minutes or until beans are tender. Serve hot, sprinkled with the parsley.

Microwave Method: Place oil in a large microwave-safe casserole dish, add onions, then cover and cook on HIGH for 3 minutes. Add prepared tomatoes, garlic, bouquet garni, tomato liquid and seasoning. Cover and cook on HIGH for 10 minutes.

Add beans and turn through the sauce to coat. Cook a further 8 to 10 minutes on HIGH or until the beans are tender. Sprinkle with parsley.

SERVES 6 TO 8

TASTY TOMATO SAUCE

30 g (1 oz) butter or dripping

1 small onion, chopped

1 small carrot, chopped

1 stalk celery, chopped

1 tablespoon plain flour

1½ cups (375 ml/12 fl oz) vegetable stock

2 tomatoes, cored and chopped

1 tablespoon tomato paste

1 small clove garlic, peeled

salt and pepper

1 teaspoon sugar

1 bay leaf

pinch dried basil

Melt butter or dripping in a saucepan, add vegetables and fry gently over a low heat until brown. Stir in the flour and cook slowly until mixture has a sandy texture, allowing it to colour slightly.

Gradually add the stock, tomatoes and tomato paste, stirring until it boils. Add garlic, salt and pepper, sugar, bay leaf and basil. Simmer uncovered for 30 to 40 minutes, then taste and adjust the seasoning if necessary. Strain the sauce, reheating it before using. Serve with steak, chops or calves' liver, or use as a base sauce for other sauces such as Chasseur Sauce (see Chicken Chasseur recipe page 79).

MAKES 2 CUPS (500 ML/16 FL OZ)

Curried Tomato Sauce with Prawns (Shrimps)

PENNE WITH TOMATO AND OLIVE SAUCE

- *1 tablespoon olive oil*
- *2 onions, finely chopped*
- *3 rashers bacon, rind removed and finely chopped*
- *8 small tomatoes, quartered*
- *2 tablespoons chopped sun-dried tomatoes*
- *2 tablespoons white wine*
- *8 black olives, pitted and chopped*
- *salt and pepper*
- *400 g to 500 g (13 oz to 16 oz) penne pasta*

Cook pasta in a large pan of boiling salted water until al dente.

Heat oil in a pan and gently fry onions until golden. Add the bacon and fry until cooked. Mix in the fresh and sun-dried tomatoes and simmer for 5 minutes or until softened.

Blend in the wine and olives, reduce heat and simmer for a few minutes or until thickened. Season with salt and pepper. Serve hot sauce over freshly cooked pasta, accompanied by a green salad.

SERVES 4

PENNE PASTA

Penne is a short, cylindrical, ridged pasta.

TOMATO COULIS WITH CRUMBED SARDINES

TOMATO COULIS

- *3 vine-ripened tomatoes, peeled, cored, seeded and finely chopped*
- *1 tablespoon chopped fresh parsley*
- *4 shallots (spring onions), thinly sliced*
- *1 tablespoon tomato paste*
- *salt and pepper*
- *2 tablespoons dry white wine*
- *4 tablespoons natural yoghurt*

CRUMBED SARDINES

- *12 to 18 sardines, cleaned and boned*
- *plain flour, seasoned with salt and pepper*
- *1 egg, beaten*
- *2 tablespoons milk*
- *120 g (4 oz) fresh breadcrumbs*
- *1 tablespoon grated Parmesan cheese*
- *olive oil*
- *lemon wedges and fresh basil, to garnish*

To Prepare Tomato Coulis: Put all ingredients into a mixing bowl and whisk together. Cover and chill until required.

To Prepare Crumbed Sardines: It is quite simple to bone a sardine. Grasp the fish by its head and gently pull down and back towards the tail. The bones will come away all attached to the head. Or cut the head off first then gently pull the backbone out. Rinse the fish clean.

Coat the sardines with seasoned flour. Combine egg and milk and dip the sardines into this mixture. Mix breadcrumbs and Parmesan cheese, then coat the sardines with this.

Heat sufficient oil in a frying pan until moderately hot and fry the sardines for 1 to 2 minutes or until golden brown, turning once carefully. Drain on paper towels. Place 3 sardines onto each entrée plate or all onto a serving plate and serve with the Tomato Coulis. Garnish with lemon wedges and fresh basil.

SERVES 4 TO 6

Left: Penne with Tomato and Olive Sauce
Right: Tomato Coulis with Crumbed Sardines

Tomato Soups

*R*ich, robust-flavoured tomato soups are enticing, whether combined with vegetables, pasta, fresh herbs or fish. Choose bright red, ripe, full-flavoured tomatoes for soup-making. The acidic-sweet balance of flavours in tomatoes makes them perfect in refreshing chilled soups for summer entertaining, too.

TOMATO AND PUMPKIN SOUP

Tomatoes add a sweeter, roundly balanced flavour as well as a bright colour to pumpkin soup.

   1 onion, finely chopped

   1 rasher bacon, finely chopped

   20 g (½ oz) butter or margarine

   2 cups mashed cooked pumpkin

   3 cups (750 ml/24 fl oz) beef stock

   400 g (13 oz) can tomatoes

   salt and pepper

   pinch ground cloves

   1 cup (250 ml/8 fl oz) milk

   chopped fresh parsley and snipped chives, to garnish

In a large pan, gently fry onion and bacon in butter until onion is soft and transparent. Add pumpkin, stock and tomatoes and simmer for 15 minutes. Mix to a purée in a food processor or blender. Return to pan and season with salt and pepper. Add cloves and milk and simmer for a few minutes.

Serve soup garnished with chopped parsley and snipped chives.

SERVES 8

OLD-FASHIONED TOMATO SOUP

   60 g (2 oz) butter or margarine

   1 stalk celery, finely chopped

   1 small carrot, finely chopped

   1 small onion, finely chopped

   1 clove garlic, crushed

   2 tablespoons cornflour

   500 g (1 lb) ripe tomatoes, skinned and chopped

   5 cups (1.25 litres/40 fl oz) beef stock

   1 bay leaf

   salt and pepper

   chopped parsley, to garnish

Heat butter in a large, heavy pan. Add celery, carrot onion and garlic. Cover and sauté for 5 minutes, shaking pan frequently. Blend cornflour with 3 tablespoons cold water, then add to pan with tomatoes and bring to the boil, stirring continuously. Add stock and bay leaf, cover, then simmer for 30 minutes. Season with salt and pepper. Remove bay leaf.

Serve soup hot, sprinkled with chopped parsley.

Variation: Stir in 150 ml (5 fl oz) cream just before serving.

SERVES 8

MINESTRONE

The borlotti beans in this recipe need to be soaked overnight before cooking.

   4 bacon rashers, rind and bones removed

   1 onion, finely chopped

   1 clove garlic, crushed

   1 stick celery, chopped

   2 potatoes, peeled and chopped

   2 carrots, peeled and sliced

   1 cup dried borlotti beans, soaked overnight

   3 tomatoes, cored and chopped

   8 cups (2 litres/64 fl oz) water or stock

   salt and pepper

   1 zucchini (courgette), sliced

   125 g (4 oz) green beans, chopped

   90 g (3 oz) shredded cabbage

   60 g (2 oz) long grain rice, washed well

   3 tablespoons chopped fresh parsley, to garnish

   grated Parmesan cheese, to garnish

Chop bacon very finely and put into a large pan with the bones and rind, onion, garlic and celery. Fry gently for 5 minutes, stirring occasionally. Add potatoes, carrots, borlotti beans and tomatoes, cover with water and add salt and pepper.

Bring to the boil, cover and simmer for 2 hours or until the beans are tender. Check the water level, adding more if necessary.

After the first hour, add the zucchini, green beans, cabbage and rice and continue simmering for 15 to 30 minutes or until rice is cooked. Remove and discard the bacon rind and bones. Check the seasoning.

Serve soup hot with the parsley and Parmesan cheese sprinkled over, accompanied by Italian bread rolls.

SERVES 6 TO 8

Pictured on previous pages: Old Fashioned Tomato Soup (page 24), Potage Pistou (page 25)

ITALIAN NOODLE SOUP

The flavours of garlic, olive oil and tomato mix to create a delicious and tempting soup.

- 2 tablespoons olive oil
- 1 rasher bacon, chopped
- 3 cloves garlic, crushed
- 250 g (8 oz) tomato, chopped
- 5 cups (1.25 litres/40 fl oz) chicken or vegetable stock
- 250 g (8 oz) linguine pasta, broken into pieces
- salt
- freshly ground black pepper
- 30 g (1 oz) Parmesan cheese, grated
- 1 tablespoon chopped fresh basil

Heat oil in a large pan and cook bacon and garlic until golden brown. Add tomato and stock, and bring to the boil. Add linguine and cook for 10 to 15 minutes or until tender. Season with salt and pepper, then stir in half the cheese and basil. Serve the soup sprinkled with the remaining cheese and basil.

SERVES 4 TO 6

NON-REACTIVE PANS

- When cooking with tomato it is best to use a non-reactive pan.

- A non-reactive pan can be stainless steel, enamel or heat proof glass, but not aluminium.

- Use of an non-reactive pan ensures that the flavours don't "react" with the pan. Such reaction can cause bitterness and discolouration of the food.

TOMATO AND SMOKED FISH SOUP

Try smoked cod, herring, kippers or mackerel in this tasty, satisfying soup.

- 30 g (1 oz) butter or margarine
- 2 smoked fish fillets, chopped
- 1 clove garlic, crushed
- 2 tablespoons plain flour
- 750 g (1½ lb) tomatoes, cored and chopped
- 2 cups (500 ml/16 fl oz) hot milk
- 1¼ cups (300 ml/10 fl oz) hot water
- salt and pepper
- ½ cup (125 ml/4 fl oz) natural yoghurt or light sour cream
- 1 tablespoon sherry, optional

Melt butter in a large pan, then stir in the fish and garlic. Add the flour and cook over medium heat, stirring for 1 minute, until foaming but not browned. Gradually add the tomatoes, milk and water, stirring constantly until it boils. Season with salt and pepper. Cover the pan and simmer for 20 minutes.

Place mixture in a food processor or blender and process until finely chopped. Add the yoghurt and sherry, if using.

Reheat without boiling and serve hot, accompanied by hot crusty bread.

SERVES 4 TO 6

POTAGE PISTOU

This recipe tastes delicious using either fresh tomatoes or quality, canned peeled tomatoes.

- 250 g (8 oz) green beans, with ends trimmed
- 625 g (1¼ lb) ripe tomatoes, peeled and chopped
- 75 g (2½ oz) egg noodles
- 1 clove garlic, crushed
- 1 tablespoon finely chopped fresh basil
- 2 tablespoons olive oil
- 1 small onion, finely chopped
- 60 g (2 oz) tasty cheese, grated
- freshly ground black pepper

Cut beans into 2.5 cm (1 in) lengths. Place 4 cups (1 litre/32 fl oz) salted water into a large pan with the chopped tomatoes and simmer for 15 minutes. Add egg noodles and green beans and cook until tender.

Combine garlic, basil, olive oil and onion and process with a little liquid until the mixture is smooth and creamy. Add to tomato and beans and simmer to heat through.

Serve soup hot, topped with grated cheese and a grinding of black pepper.

SERVES 6

Skim solidified fat from chilled soup.

For every 2 cups of soup, use shells and whites of 3 eggs and ¼ cup (60 ml/ 2 fl oz) white wine.

As soon as the mixture looks milky, stop whisking.

Make a small hole in the froth.

Place a scalded tea towel over a clean bowl and carefully pour the consommé into it.

Tomato Consommé

TOMATO CONSOMME

- *6 cups (1.5 litres/48 fl oz) home-made chicken or beef stock*
- *8 large ripe tomatoes, peeled, cored and chopped*
- *1 bacon bone*
- *1 teaspoon lemon juice*
- *1 teaspoon tarragon-flavoured wine vinegar*
- *eggs (refer method for details of the number of eggs you will need)*
- *white wine (refer method for details of the amount of white wine you will need)*
- *freshly ground black pepper*

Put the stock, tomatoes, bacon bone, lemon juice and vinegar into a large pan, cover and bring to the boil. Simmer for 1 hour then strain and cool. Refrigerate to let the fat set on top.

Remove fat and measure the soup. For every 2 cups (500 ml/16 fl oz) of soup add the shells and whites of 3 eggs and ¼ cup (60 ml/2 fl oz) white wine and bring to the boil, whisking constantly. This collects impurities, leaving the liquid sparkling clear. This should take about 10 minutes.

As soon as the mixture looks milky, stop whisking. If you continue, you will prevent the egg filter forming. Let the filter of egg white rise slowly to the top of the pan, then turn down the heat.

With a ladle or spoon handle, make a small hole in the froth so the consommé bubbles through the filter only in that place. Simmer gently for 30 minutes.

Place a scalded fine linen tea towel over a clean bowl and carefully ladle the consommé into it, sliding out the filter intact. Do not press on the mixture in the towel. If consommé is not sparkling clear, it can be strained through the cloth and filtered again.

Reheat the consommé in a clean pan and serve at a gourmet dinner party.

SERVES 8

Right: Grilled Tomato and Red Pepper Soup (see recipe page 28)

TOMATO AND VEGETABLE SOUP

30 g (1 oz) butter or margarine

2 large onions, chopped

1 kg (2 lb) tomatoes, cored and chopped

2 carrots, sliced

1 large potato, peeled and thinly sliced

½ cup (125 ml/4 fl oz) tomato paste

2 cups (500 ml/16 fl oz) chicken stock

freshly ground black pepper

grated Parmesan cheese or croutons, to garnish

Melt butter in a large pan and gently fry onions for 2 minutes, stirring occasionally, until lightly browned. Add the remaining ingredients, bring to the boil, then reduce heat and simmer for 30 minutes or until the vegetables are tender.

Purée the soup in a food processor or blender. Reheat and adjust seasoning. Serve soup hot, sprinkled with Parmesan cheese or croutons.

SERVES 6

GRILLED TOMATO AND RED PEPPER SOUP

Pictured on page 27.

Grilling the tomatoes gives this soup a particularly delicious flavour.

1 kg (2 lb) ripe tomatoes

2 large red capsicums (peppers)

2 tablespoons olive oil

1 large onion, finely chopped

3 cups (750 ml/24 fl oz) vegetable or chicken stock

salt and pepper

light sour cream, to garnish

Core the tomatoes and score around the outside. Cut capsicum (peppers) in half lengthways and remove seeds. Place tomatoes and capsicum (peppers) under a red-hot grill until skins are blackened, turning tomatoes over to blacken both sides. Remove skins from tomatoes and capsicum (peppers). The capsicum (pepper) can be rinsed under the tap to remove any remaining black skin. Dry throughly. Mix tomatoes to a purée in a food processor or blender.

Heat oil in a large pan and gently fry onion until soft. Add tomatoes and simmer for 10 minutes. Add stock and return to the boil.

Mix the pepper to a purée, add to the soup and simmer for a few minutes. Season with salt and pepper.

Serve soup hot or chilled, with a tablespoon of light sour cream added to each portion.

SERVES 6

TOMATO FENNEL SOUP

3 fennel bulbs

90 g (3 oz) butter or margarine

1 large onion, chopped

3 cloves garlic, crushed

salt and pepper

1.6 kg (3¼ lb) can Italian tomatoes

3 tablespoons Pernod

2 cups (500 ml/16 fl oz) well-flavoured chicken stock

2 tablespoons chopped fennel tops, to garnish

pitta bread

Trim fennel and coarsely chop two bulbs. Melt 60 g (2 oz) butter in a large pan, add chopped fennel, onion and garlic and gently fry until softened. Season with salt and pepper. Add tomatoes and juice, cover and cook over low heat for 30 minutes.

Purée vegetables and return them to pan. Finely chop remaining fennel bulb. Cook in butter for 5 minutes. Add to purée with Pernod and chicken stock. Heat through gently to boiling point.

Serve soup sprinkled with chopped fennel tops in heated bowls, accompanied by triangles of pitta bread, toasted, buttered and sprinkled with herbs.

SERVES 6

FENNEL

Fennel has a bulbous, pale green to white body, similar to celery and light feathery leaves. It has a strong anise flavour.

ORANGE AND CREAMY TOMATO SOUP

850 ml (28 fl oz) tomato juice, well chilled

1 cup (250 ml/8 fl oz) freshly squeezed orange juice

1 tablespoon orange rind

1 tablespoon finely chopped chives

1 cup (250 ml/8 fl oz) cream

freshly ground black pepper

1 avocado

1 tablespoon lemon juice

snipped chives, extra, to garnish

Blend tomato juice, orange juice and rind, chives and fresh cream. Season with pepper. Peel and seed avocado, slice it thinly and sprinkle a little lemon juice over it to prevent discolouration. Serve the soup in individual soup bowls. Float the avocado slices on top and garnish with chives.

SERVES 4

CHILLED TOMATO DILL SOUP

6 large ripe tomatoes, cored and sliced

1 medium to large onion, sliced

1 clove garlic, crushed

1 pinch salt

freshly ground black pepper

2 tablespoons tomato paste

¼ cup (60 ml/2 fl oz) water

6 sprigs fresh dill

1 cup (250 ml/8 fl oz) chicken stock

¾ cup (185 ml/6 fl oz) fresh cream

small sprigs fresh dill, extra, to garnish

In a medium-sized pan combine tomatoes, onion, garlic, salt, pepper, tomato paste, water and dill. Cover and cook over medium heat for about 10 minutes or until tomatoes have softened.

Process mixture in a food processor or blender with the stock and cream until smooth. Pour into a large bowl, cover and refrigerate until chilled. Ladle into chilled soup bowls and serve garnished with dill and accompanied by grissini bread sticks.

SERVES 6

GAZPACHO

A popular, refreshing chilled soup to liven jaded palates during a heat wave. Use a food processor to chop the tomatoes, cucumbers, onion and capsicum (pepper) to save time.

1 kg (2 lb) tomatoes, cored, peeled and finely chopped

2 medium-sized cucumbers, peeled, seeded and finely chopped

1 red Spanish onion, finely chopped

1 red or green capsicum (pepper), seeded and finely chopped

2 cloves garlic, crushed

3 tablespoons olive oil

3 tablespoons white wine vinegar

salt and pepper

pinch cayenne pepper

1½ cups (375 ml/12 fl oz) tomato juice

snipped chives, to garnish

After chopping the tomatoes, cucumbers, onion and capsicum (pepper), transfer them to a bowl and add garlic. Stir in the olive oil, vinegar, salt and pepper, cayenne and tomato juice. Stir well, then cover and refrigerate until well chilled.

Serve soup cold, garnished with chives.

SERVES 8

NO-COOK TOMATO SOUP

This ice cold soup, enriched with vitamins and fibre, gives a refreshing lift on hot days.

750 g (1½ lb) tomatoes, cored and chopped

60 g (2 oz) seeded cucumber, finely chopped

1 small onion, finely chopped

1 small stick celery, thinly sliced

1 teaspoon sugar

1 clove garlic, crushed

¼ teaspoon salt

2 drops Tabasco sauce

Mix the tomatoes in a food processor or blender to form a purée. Stir in the remaining ingredients and refrigerate until required. Serve chilled.

SERVES 4

TO SEED A CUCUMBER

To seed a cucumber, cut it in half lengthwise and run a metal spoon down the middle to scrape out the seeds.

Pizzas and Pies

*T*reat your family and friends to the sunny taste of Mediterranean cuisine with one of these delicious pizzas or delightful pies. The aroma of home-made pizzas and pies featuring the popular tomato is irresistible. These recipes appeal to the eyes as well as the appetite!

WHOLEMEAL PIZZA DOUGH

625 g (21 oz) wholemeal self-raising flour

pinch of salt and pepper

60 g (2 oz) butter or margarine

1½ cups (375 ml/12 fl oz) cold water

Sift the flour, salt and pepper into a mixing bowl, then rub in the butter until the mixture resembles coarse breadcrumbs. Make a well in the centre, pour in the water and mix with a round-bladed knife to form a firm dough. Knead lightly for 1 to 2 minutes, then divide the dough in half.

Roll out each portion to fit a lightly oiled 28 cm to 30 cm (11 in to 12 in) pizza tray, and top with one of the pizza variations detailed below.

MAKES 2 PIZZA BASES

ANCHOVIES

If you find the flavour of anchovies a little too strong, soak them in milk for about 10 minutes before using them. This reduces the saltiness and the strength of their taste a little, but retains some of the Mediterranean flavour that is so unique.

TOMATO, ARTICHOKE AND ANCHOVY PIZZAS

These individual pizzas, using convenient pitta pocket breads, are simple to make and even simpler to serve.

4 Egyptian oval pitta breads or similar wholemeal pitta pocket breads

1 cup (250 ml/8 fl oz) Napoletana Sauce (see recipe page 15)

250 g (8 oz) jar preserved artichoke hearts, drained

45 g (1½ oz) can anchovy fillets, drained

2 teaspoons capers

4 tablespoons grated Parmesan cheese

Preheat oven to 200°C (400°F).

Place pitta breads on a baking tray and heat in an oven for 5 minutes. Spread Napoletana Sauce over the warm breads and top each attractively with a quarter of the artichoke hearts and anchovies. Sprinkle ½ teaspoon capers and 1 tablespoon grated Parmesan cheese over each. Return to oven and bake for a further 5 minutes.

Serve pizzas hot, accompanied by a mixed salad, for a delicious quick meal.

SERVES 4

TOMATO AND CARROT FILO PIE

16 sheets filo pastry (use ready-made pastry for this recipe)

90 g (3 oz) butter or margarine, melted

FILLING

3 onions, sliced

½ cup (125 ml/4 fl oz) vegetable or macadamia nut oil

4 carrots, grated

2 tomatoes, skinned and chopped

2 tablespoons tomato paste

4 teaspoons hot chilli paste

salt

Preheat oven to 180°C (350°F).

Line a 23 cm (9 in) flan tin or ceramic quiche dish with 8 sheets of filo pastry, brushing each layer with melted butter. Trim edges with kitchen scissors.

To Prepare Filling: In a large frying pan, gently fry onion in half the oil until soft and transparent. Remove with a slotted spoon, leaving as much oil in pan as possible. Add remaining oil to pan then gently fry carrots until soft. Add tomatoes, tomato paste, hot chilli paste and onions and simmer for 5 minutes. Add salt.

To Assemble Pie: Place tomato and carrot mixture into filo-lined flan tin. Brush remaining layers of filo pastry with melted butter and place on top of filling. Trim edges neatly with kitchen scissors and brush top of pie with melted butter.

Bake for 30 minutes, or until cooked.

SERVES 4 TO 6

Pictured on previous pages: Tomato, Artichoke and Anchovy Pizzas (page 32), Tomato and Onion Tart Niçoise (page 38)

Tomato and Carrot Filo Pie

VEGETARIAN PIZZA

3 tablespoons olive oil

1 small (about 250 g (8 oz)) eggplant (aubergine), cut into 1 cm (½ in) cubes

½ quantity Wholemeal Pizza Dough (see recipe page 32)

1 cup (250 ml/8 fl oz) Napoletana Sauce (see recipe page 15)

185 g (6 oz) mozzarella cheese, grated

1 cup cauliflower florets

60 g (2 oz) mushrooms, sliced

unsweetened pinapple pieces

2 small zucchini (courgettes), cut into thin rings

¼ red capsicum (pepper), cut into strips

¼ green capsicum (pepper), cut into strips

12 black olives, pitted

salt and pepper

Preheat oven to 190°C (375°F).

Heat oil in a frying pan and fry eggplant until golden.

Drain well on paper towels.

Spread the prepared pizza dough with the Napoletana sauce and cover it with two-thirds of the grated cheese. Top with the eggplant, cauliflower, mushrooms, pineapple, zucchini, capsicum, olives and remaining cheese. Season with salt and pepper.

Bake for 25 to 30 minutes, or until the dough is well risen and golden and the topping is cooked.

Serve pizza hot, cut into portions.

SERVES 2 TO 4

PIZZA MARINARA

1 quantity Wholemeal Pizza Dough (see recipe page 32)

Napoletana Sauce (see recipe page 15)

185 g (6 oz) mozzarella cheese

250 g (8 oz) small green prawns (shrimps) peeled and deveined

250 g (8 oz) thick fish fillets, sliced

12 mussels, shelled

12 smoked or fresh oysters

salt and pepper

4 shallots (spring onions), thinly sliced

2 tablespoons finely chopped parsley

lemon wedges, to garnish

Preheat oven to 190°C (375°F).

Spread the two prepared pizza doughs with the Napoletana Sauce, then cover with the grated cheese. Arrange the prawns (shrimps) and fish over the cheese. Spread the mussels and oysters over the fish and season with salt and pepper. Sprinkle the shallots and parsley over the top. Bake for 10 minutes, then reduce the temperature to 175°C (345°F) and bake for 10 to 15 minutes more.

Serve pizzas hot, cut in portions and garnished with lemon wedges.

SERVES 4 TO 8

TOMATO AND FRESH SARDINE PIZZA

½ quantity Wholemeal Pizza Dough (see recipe page 32)

4 tablespoons tomato paste

500 g (1 lb) fresh sardines

2 tablespoons olive oil

8 fresh sage leaves

45 g (1½ oz) canned anchovy fillets

30 g (1 oz) butter or margarine

4 tablespoons grated Parmesan cheese

Preheat oven to 220°C (425°F).

Roll pizza dough out and line a 28 cm to 30 cm (11 in to 12 in) pizza tray. Spread dough with tomato paste.

Cut heads off sardines and pull backbones out from head to tail. Rinse sardines and dry well. Brush oil over pizza dough and arrange sardines in 2 circles (outer and inner) on top. Place sage leaves on top around edge and place an anchovy over each sage leaf. Slice butter thinly and place on top of fish. Sprinkle with grated Parmesan cheese.

Bake for 15 to 20 minutes, or until cooked. Serve hot with a tossed salad.

SERVES 2 TO 4

Pizza Marinara (back)
Vegetarian Pizza (front)

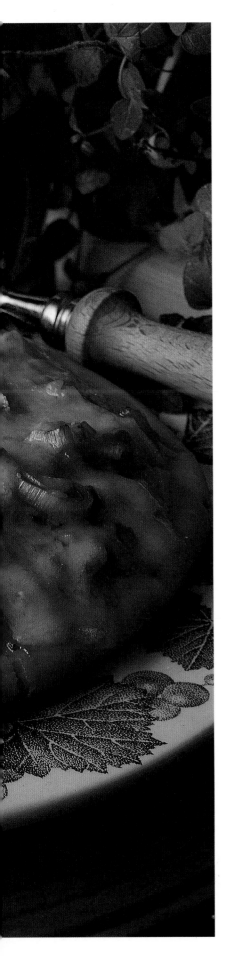

SPEEDY PIZZA NAPOLITANA

Use a frozen or pre-cooked pizza base for convenience when making this tasty traditional pizza. Home-made or processed Napolitana sauce may be used.

  1 frozen or pre-cooked pizza base

  1 leek, sliced or 1 large onion, chopped

  1 tablespoon olive oil

  1 cup (250 ml/8 fl oz) Napolitana Sauce (see recipe page 15)

  125 g (4 oz) tasty cheese, grated

  4 tablespoons grated Parmesan cheese

Preheat oven to 200°C (400°F).

Prepare pizza base according to directions on packet. For best results, heat uncooked pizza base in an oven for at least 5 minutes before adding topping.

Gently fry leek or onion in olive oil until soft. Add Napolitana Sauce and heat through. Spread hot mixture over the hot pizza base and sprinkle with the cheeses. Bake for 5 minutes, or until cheese is golden.

Serve pizza immediately, with a green salad.

SERVES 2 TO 4 (ACCORDING TO APPETITE!)

MIXED TOMATO TART

BASE

  1 teaspoon active dry yeast

  pinch sugar

  ⅔ cup (160 ml/5 fl oz) warm water

  250 g (8 oz) plain flour

  ¼ cup (60 ml/2 fl oz) olive oil

MIXED TOMATO FILLING

  50 g cherry tomatoes, halved

  4 plum tomatoes, cut into wedges

  1 red onion, sliced

  2 tablespoons balsamic vinegar

  2 tablespoons chopped thyme

  freshly ground black pepper

To Prepare Base: Place yeast, sugar and water in a bowl and set aside in a warm place until foamy.

Add flour and oil and mix to a smooth dough. Knead dough on a lightly floured surface until smooth and elastic. Place in a lightly oiled bowl, cover and stand in a warm place until doubled in size.

Preheat oven to 180°C (350°F).

Press out dough to form a round and pinch the edge between thumb and forefinger to make a patterned edge.

Place on a lightly oiled oven tray and bake for 20 minutes or until golden. Cool.

To Prepare Filling: Combine tomatoes, onion, vinegar, thyme and pepper. Spoon into prepared pastry shell and serve in wedges with mixed salad greens.

SERVES 6

Speedy Pizza Napolitana

TOMATO AND ONION TART NICOISE

Pictured on pages 30-31.

PASTRY

250 g (8 oz) Pâté Brisée (see Onion and Blue Cheese Quiches recipe page 41)

FILLING

500 g (1 lb) onions, thinly sliced

½ cup (125 ml/4 fl oz) olive oil

½ teaspoon salt

freshly ground black pepper

500 g (1 lb) vine-ripened tomatoes

2 tablespoons chopped fresh oregano or marjoram

8 pitted black olives

Preheat oven to 200°C (400°F).

Roll pastry out and line a 23 cm (9 in) flan tin. Bake blind for 10 minutes.

To Prepare Filling: Gently fry onions in oil in a large, heavy-based, covered frying pan for 20 to 30 minutes, or until soft, lightly coloured and very limp. Drain onion in a sieve and reserve the oil. Season onions with salt and pepper. Slice tomatoes 1 cm (½ in) thick.

To Assemble Tart: Spread onions in pastry case. Arrange overlapping slices of tomato around the edge, then arrange an inside row meeting in the centre. Brush reserved oil over the tomatoes and sprinkle with half the oregano or marjoram. Bake for 30 minutes or until cooked, brushing with more oil if tomatoes look dry.

Arrange olives around edge of tart and sprinkle with remaining oregano.

Serve warm, with a green salad.

SERVES 4 TO 6

CHEESE AND TOMATO QUICHE LORRAINE

1 sheet ready-made short crust pastry

6 rashers bacon, rind and bones removed

1 tomato

125 g (4 oz) grated tasty cheese

3 eggs

1½ cups (375 ml/12 fl oz) milk

3 tablespoons chopped fresh parsley

salt and pepper

Preheat oven to 180°C (350°F).

Line a 23 cm (9 in) flan tin with the prepared pastry. Fry bacon until crisp, then crumble into small pieces.

Cut tomato into 8 wedges and arrange them in a circle in the pastry case. Sprinkle with bacon and cheese.

Beat eggs, milk and parsley together. Season with salt and pepper, then pour over the tomato, bacon and cheese.

Bake for 30 minutes, or until custard has set.

Serve hot, accompanied by a green salad.

SERVES 4 TO 6

PIPERADE PIE

PASTRY

310 g (10 oz) plain wholemeal flour

125 g (4 oz) butter or margarine, diced

cold water, to mix

FILLING

2 large ripe tomatoes

1 red capsicum (pepper)

60 g (2 oz) butter or margarine

4 shallots (spring onions) cut into 1 cm (½ in) lengths

1 clove garlic, crushed

4 eggs, beaten

2 tablespoons shredded, fresh basil

salt and pepper

To Prepare Pastry: Sift flour then place in a food processor. Add butter and process until the texture resembles breadcrumbs. Add sufficient cold water, gradually, and mix until a dough forms which leaves the sides of the processor bowl. Turn onto a lightly floured surface and shape into a flat round cake. Wrap in greaseproof paper and chill for at least 15 minutes.

Preheat oven to 200°C (400°F).

To Prepare Filling: Blanch tomatoes, remove skin, cut in half and squeeze out seeds. Chop tomatoes. Deseed capsicum and blanch, then slice into short, thin strips. Heat butter in a frying pan and gently fry shallots and garlic until soft. Add capsicum (pepper) and cook for 5 minutes. Add tomatoes and simmer for 1 minute.

To Prepare Pie: Roll pastry out and line a 23 cm (9 in) flan tin. Line the pastry with greaseproof paper and dried beans or rice and bake blind for 10 minutes. Reduce oven temperature to 175°C (350°F). Remove paper and beans. Pour tomato mixture into pastry case. Beat eggs with basil and season with salt and pepper. Pour over tomato mixture. Return to oven and cook for a further 10 minutes, or until set.

Serve pie hot or cold, with salad.

SERVES 4

Piperade Pie

Using fingertips, rub the butter into the flour.

Gradually stir in the water and egg yolk, using a knife.

Lightly knead the dough to form a smooth ball.

Roll the dough out on a lightly floured surface.

Onion and Blue Cheese Quiches

ONION AND BLUE CHEESE QUICHES

PATE BRISEE

> 250 g (8 oz) plain flour
> 185 g (6 oz) butter
> 2 egg yolks
> cold water, to mix

FILLING

> 2 tablespoons olive oil
> 1 onion, chopped
> 1 clove garlic, crushed
> 3 tomatoes, chopped
> 1 teaspoon chopped fresh oregano
> freshly ground black pepper

> 3 eggs, beaten
> 125 g (4 oz) blue vein cheese, crumbled
> 30 g (1 oz) grated Parmesan cheese
> 4 to 6 mignonette lettuce leaves and cherry tomatoes, to garnish

To Prepare Pâté Brisée: Sift flour into a bowl, then rub in butter until mixture resembles breadcrumbs. Add egg yolks and just enough water to form a firm dough. Pastry may be made in a food processor up to this stage. Knead quickly on a floured board, just until pastry is smooth underneath. Wrap in greaseproof paper and chill in the refrigerator for 20 minutes.

Preheat oven to 200°C (400°F).

To Prepare Filling: Heat oil in a pan and fry onion and garlic until soft and transparent. Mix in tomatoes, oregano, pepper, eggs and blue vein cheese.

To Assemble Quiches: Roll pastry out thinly and cut to fit 4 to 6 individual quiche tins or ceramic dishes. Bake blind for 10 minutes. Pour filling into pastry cases. Bake for another 10 minutes, then sprinkle the Parmesan cheese over the top. Reduce oven temperature to 180°C (350°F) and continue baking for 20 to 30 minutes, or until the top is golden and set.

Serve quiches hot, on individual entrée plates, garnished with lettuce and cherry tomatoes.

SERVES 4 TO 6

PISSALADIERE

SHORT CRUST PASTRY

250 g (8 oz) plain flour

60 g (2 oz) butter, diced

60 g (2 oz) lard, diced

3 to 6 tablespoons iced water

TOPPING

3 tablespoons olive oil

2 large onions, thinly sliced

1 clove garlic, crushed

500 g (1 lb) tomatoes, cored, peeled and sliced

freshly ground black pepper

60 g (2 oz) canned anchovies, drained

2 tablespoons milk

12 large black olives, halved and pitted or 24 small olives, whole

olive oil, extra

Preheat oven to 200°C (400°F).

To Prepare Short Crust Pastry: Sift flour into a mixing bowl. Add butter and lard and rub in quickly with the fingertips until the mixture resembles fine breadcrumbs. Add just enough water to make the dough smooth and pliable. The pastry may be made in a food processor up to this stage. Turn onto a floured surface and knead gently for a few seconds or until smooth underneath. Roll out to fit a greased 18 cm x 28 cm (7 in x 11 in) Swiss roll tin. Line the tin with pastry and refrigerate until required.

To Prepare Topping: Heat oil in a large pan and gently fry onions and garlic for 10 minutes. Spread mixture over the dough, then top with tomatoes. Season lightly with pepper. Rinse anchovies in milk to remove excess salt. Drain well. Arrange anchovies over tomatoes in a lattice pattern and fill the diamonds created with the olives. Brush lightly with extra olive oil and bake for 25 to 30 minutes.

Variations: Cover tomatoes with salami slices and decorate with strips of cheese.

SERVES 4 TO 6

Pissaladière

TOMATO AND GRUYERE QUICHE

Quiches are always superb for light luncheons and picnics, especially if served with crisp green salads and chilled white wine.

> 750 g (1½ lb) firm ripe tomatoes, cored, peeled and chopped
>
> salt and pepper
>
> 375 g (12 oz) packet frozen puff pastry, thawed
>
> 125 g (4 oz) Gruyère cheese, grated
>
> ½ cup (125 ml/4 fl oz) cream
>
> 2 eggs
>
> pinch dried basil
>
> salt and pepper, extra

Preheat oven to 230°C (450°F).

Place a baking tray in the oven to heat. Drain tomatoes in a colander and season with salt and pepper. Roll out pastry thinly, and line a 23 cm (9 in) flan tin, then sprinkle half the grated cheese over the top.

Beat the cream, eggs, basil, salt and pepper together. Spoon tomatoes into pastry case, spreading them out evenly, then pour in the egg mixture. Pastry off-cuts can be cut into strips and used to give a lattice top to the quiche.

Place the quiche on the preheated baking tray and bake for 5 minutes. Reduce temperature to 200°C (400°F) and bake for a further 5 minutes. Lower temperature to 180°C (350°F) and continue baking for another 20 minutes, or until filling is puffed and golden. If pastry browns before filling has set, cover the top with a piece of aluminium foil.

Serve quiche hot (while still puffed), for the best result.

SERVES 4 TO 6

ITALIAN EGGPLANT AND TOMATO PIE

This delicious vegetarian dish can be prepared in advance and then baked when required.

> 1 kg (2 lb) small to medium eggplant (aubergine), sliced
>
> salt
>
> flour, seasoned with salt and pepper
>
> ½ cup (125 ml/4 fl oz) olive oil
>
> 375 g (12 oz) mozzarella cheese, sliced
>
> ¾ cup (185 ml/6 fl oz) Napoletana Sauce (see recipe page 15)
>
> 60 g (2 oz) freshly grated Parmesan cheese

Preheat oven to 180°C (350°F).

Sprinkle eggplant (aubergine) with salt and leave for 30 minutes. Sprinkle the slices with seasoned flour. Heat half the oil in a frying pan and fry eggplant in batches until softened, adding more oil to pan if necessary. Drain eggplant on paper towels.

Lightly grease a deep cake tin or soufflé dish, about 18 cm to 20 cm (7 in to 8 in) diameter. Make layers of eggplant, mozzarella and Napoletana Sauce, starting with eggplant and finishing with sauce, seasoning each layer with salt and pepper. Top with the Parmesan cheese then bake for 30 minutes.

Serve hot, cut into wedges and accompanied by rice or risoni (rice-shaped pasta).

SERVES 6 TO 8

TOMATO AND ANCHOVY FLAN

> 250 g (8 oz) Pâté Brisée (see Onion and Blue Cheese Quiches recipe page 41)

FILLING

> 185 g (6 oz) tasty cheese, grated
>
> 2 eggs, lightly beaten
>
> 1 tablespoon plain flour or semolina
>
> 1 cup (250 ml/8 fl oz) milk
>
> salt and freshly ground pepper
>
> 2 tomatoes, skinned and sliced
>
> 30 g (1 oz) butter or margarine
>
> 8 anchovy fillets

Preheat oven to 190°C (375°F).

Roll out pastry and line a 23 cm (9 in) flan tin. Bake pastry blind for 15 minutes. Remove and cool slightly. Reduce oven temperature to 180°C (350°F).

To Prepare Filling: Combine cheese, eggs, flour and milk. Spread over the base of the pastry case and season with salt and pepper. Arrange tomatoes over the filling in an overlapping pattern. Dot with butter and anchovies and bake for 20 to 30 minutes, or until the filling has set.

Serve hot or cold, with a tossed salad.

SERVES 4

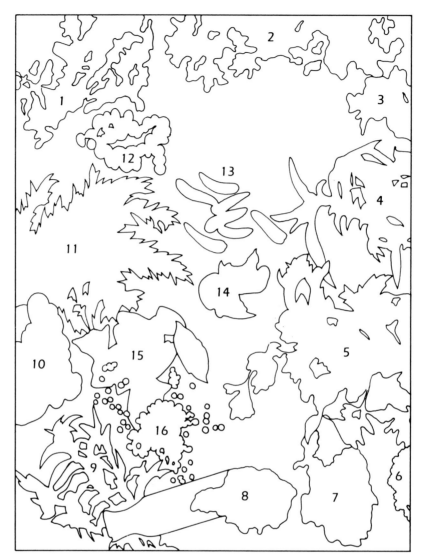

1 Watercress 2 Marjoram 3 Mint 4 Sage 5 Continental parsley 6 Parsley
7 Curry powder 8 Chilli powder 9 Tarragon 10 Ginger root 11 Dill
12 Capers 13 Chillies 14 Garlic 15 Bay leaves 16 Black peppercorns

Herbs, Spices and Flavourings

*A*lthough the tomato needs no more than a touch of salt, pepper and sugar to bring out its
incomparable sweet and sour flavouring, every culture has its favourite
additions, whether serving the fruit raw or cooked.
Fresh herbs like basil, oregano, tarragon, chives, sage, dill and parsley all subtly enhance its personality
and provide an interesting visual contrast with their differing shapes and colours. Chilli, capers,
ginger, curry and mustard also make flavoursome and sometimes piquant additions.
Garlic is a natural accompaniment to tomato, as are olive oil, cream, yoghurt
and cheese, all of which add texture as well as flavour.

Salads and Juices

*T*omatoes can be served in practically every salad imaginable, salad entrées, side salads, accompanying salads and main course salads. Use succulent vine-ripened tomatoes or dainty and delicious cherry tomatoes and simply let the flavours speak for themselves. Home-made tomato juices can also be prepared in many refreshing ways.

CHERRY TOMATO AND BASIL SALAD

Sweet basil and tomatoes are garden friends, the herb protecting the fruit from disease and insects. Tomatoes sprinkled with basil make a colourful and piquant salad.

2 punnets cherry tomatoes, washed and dried

4 tablespoons French Dressing (see recipe page 57)

finely grated rind of 1 lemon or 2 limes

1 tablespoon shredded fresh basil leaves

Slice tomatoes in half through the flower centre, not through the stalk centre. Place the tomatoes in a salad bowl.

Pour the chilled dressing over the tomatoes and stir lightly until coated. Sprinkle with lemon rind and fresh basil.

Delicious with sliced cooked ham, cold chicken and turkey and an essential salad in a cold buffet menu.

SERVES 6 TO 8

TOMATO AND YOGHURT SALAD

This light and summery salad is low in kilojoules and makes a refreshing accompaniment to barbecued fish or fresh prawns (shrimps).

4 tablespoons natural yoghurt

1 tablespoon mayonnaise

2 teaspoons chopped fresh coriander

1 tablespoon chopped shallots (spring onions)

1 teaspoon finely chopped ginger

1 tablespoon shredded lemon grass

2 teaspoons lemon or lime juice

freshly ground black pepper

3 large ripe tomatoes, sliced

fresh coriander, extra, to garnish

Blend together yoghurt, mayonnaise, coriander, shallots, ginger, lemon grass, lemon juice and pepper. Cover and refrigerate until required. Meanwhile, arrange the tomato slices in an overlapping pattern on a serving platter. Just before serving, spoon over the yoghurt dressing and garnish with coriander.

SERVES 6

TOMATO AND AVOCADO SHELLS

A perfect accompaniment to poached salmon or trout.

6 medium-sized vine-ripened tomatoes

salt and pepper

2 large ripe avocados, chopped

3 tablespoons French Dressing (see recipe, page 57)

juice of ½ lemon

2 tablespoons thinly sliced shallots (spring onions)

1 tablespoon chopped fresh dill or fennel

Slice off the round end of the tomatoes and scoop out the seeds and membranes. Season shell with salt and pepper, invert and leave to drain.

Combine the avocado with the remaining ingredients. Cover and chill for 30 minutes.

Spoon the avocado mixture into the tomato shells and serve with poached salmon or as a salad entrée accompanied by mixed cress salad greens or snow pea sprouts.

SERVES 6

Pictured on previous pages: Cherry Tomato and Basil Salad (page 48), Tomatoes Vinaigrette (page 56)

Tomato and Avocado Shells

Storage and Preparation of Salad Vegetables

Name	Storage	Preparation
Alfalfa sprouts	Keep refrigerated as they continue to grow.	Simply pull required amount from punnet.
Asparagus	Refrigerate in a plastic bag for 2 to 3 days.	Blanch in boiling, salted water and refresh before using or simply steam lightly.
Avocado	Store at room temperature until ripe then refrigerate for up to 3 days.	Eat at room temperature for full flavour. Slice just before using — otherwise rub the cut surfaces with lemon juice or vinaigrette.
Bean sprouts	Refrigerate for up to 7 days.	Pinch off the dry, stringy end of the root before using.
Capsicum (peppers)	Refrigerate in crisper for up to 10 days.	Use raw or char the skin and use cooked. Halve, remove seeds and woody stem. Slice or chop.
Celery	Refrigerate in a plastic bag for up to 7 days.	May be sliced or cut into sticks. For celery curls, split 6 cm (2½ in) lengths halfway down each piece a few times. Repeat at other end and plunge into iced water. Leave until curled and crisp.
CUCUMBERS Apple cucumber	Wash and dry, store in crisper in refrigerator for up to 7 days.	Peel before using.
Green or ridge cucumber	Wash and dry, store in crisper in refrigerator for up to 7 days.	Peel, leaving a little of the green skin (this is said to help with digestion). The surface may be scored with a fork. May be sliced into rounds or halved and seeded then sliced. Some people still like to lightly salt the slices to remove indigestible juices. Allow to stand for 30 minutes, drain and rinse well with cold water.
Lebanese cucumber	Wash and dry, store in crisper in refrigerator for up to 7 days.	Chop and use in salads.
Telegraph cucumber	Wash and dry, store in crisper in refrigerator for up to 7 days.	Chop and use in salads.
ONIONS Shallot (scallion, sometimes called green onions)	Refrigerate in a crisper.	Trim away roots and peel dry outer leaves before using.
Spring onion	Refrigerate in a crisper.	Use white bulb with a little of the green stem finely chopped.
Spanish onion	Refrigerate in a crisper.	Peel outer leaves, chop or slice and add to salad.
True French shallot	Refrigerate in a crisper.	Used mainly in sautés.
White onions	Store in a cool, dry, dark place.	Peel before use. Use sparingly.

Flavours of Salad Greens

Name	Description	Flavour
Chicory (Belgian endive or whitloof)	Tightly clustered, smooth white leaves with yellow tips.	Slightly bitter
Curly endive	Sold in large bunches. The long leaves graduate from pale, greeny yellow to dark green. Use only the paler heart and stalks.	Bitter
Escarole	Long frilly leaves. Use only the centre young leaves.	Slightly bitter
Butter lettuce (round lettuce)	Soft, smallish lettuce.	Mild
Cos or Romaine lettuce	Elongated head of dark green oval leaves and a crisp pale green heart.	Slightly pungent
Iceberg or crisp head lettuce	A large lettuce with crisp outer leaves and a firm sweet heart. This is the basis of many a salad as the leaves will stay crisp.	Sweet, mild
Mignonette lettuce	Soft, smallish leaves with edges tinged pink to red.	Slightly bitter
Mustard and cress	Seeds are usually sown together and eaten at the seedling stage. Sold in punnets. Snip off the tops as required.	Hot and peppery
Radicchio	Sold as tiny, single loose leaves either wholly green or tinged with red. Some varieties come as a slightly conical head.	Slightly bitter
Rocket	Small, acidic, dark green leaves. Sold while the plant is still very young.	Acidic
Silverbeet	Often called spinach. Use in salads only when leaves are very young. Discard the white stalk. The older, larger leaves should be steamed and eaten hot.	Mild
Spinach (English)	Dark green leaves. Eaten raw in salads when leaves are young and fresh. Stalk may be eaten as well.	Mild
Watercress	Pick over the bunch using only young leaves and tender stems for salads. Whatever remains will make an excellent soup.	Pungent, slightly peppery

BOCCONCINI AND TOMATO SALAD

4 bocconcini cheeses

1 punnet cherry or tear drop tomatoes

4 tablespoons French Dressing (see recipe page 57), made with balsamic vinegar

2 tablespoons chopped sun-dried tomatoes

4 tablespoons shredded fresh basil

watercress sprigs or snow pea sprouts, to garnish

Slice each cheese into 5 mm (¼ in) thick slices and arrange on four entrée plates. Cut tomatoes in half through flower, not down through stalk. Gently fold cherry tomatoes with dressing and sun-dried tomatoes until well coated. Divide tomato mixture between the four plates. Sprinkle each salad with 1 tablespoon shredded basil. Chill slightly before serving.

Serve as a salad entrée, garnished with watercress or snow peas sprouts.

SERVES 4

Bocconcini and Tomato Salad

TOMATO AND RICOTTA SALAD

- 4 vine-ripened tomatoes
- salt and pepper
- 250 g (8 oz) ricotta cheese
- 3 tablespoons cream
- 2 tablespoons snipped chives
- 2 tablespoons sliced shallots (spring onions)
- 1 clove garlic, crushed
- 4 tablespoons French Dressing or Tomato Flavoured Oil (see recipes pages 57 and 86)
- salad greens or snow pea sprouts, to garnish

Blanch and skin tomatoes. Cut a slice from the top (not the stem end) of each tomato and scoop out seeds with a metal teaspoon, leaving fleshy membrane intact. Sprinkle inside of tomatoes with salt and pepper, turn over and leave to drain.

Mix ricotta cheese with cream, chives, shallots and garlic and spoon into the hollow tomatoes. Place on individual entrée plates and spoon dressing over each one.

Serve as an entrée or light meal, accompanied by salad greens.

SERVES 4

SALTING EGGPLANT

When eggplant (aubergine) is sliced and salted, it is called degorging. This process draws out moisture and bitterness.

RATATOUILLE

The flavour of this dish will develop and improve on keeping. Prepare and store in the refrigerator. Ratatouille may be served warm or chilled.

- 3 small, (about 500 g (1 lb)) eggplants (aubergines)
- salt
- ½ cup (125 ml/4 fl oz) olive oil
- 3 onions, thinly sliced
- 2 cloves garlic, crushed
- 500 g (1 lb) zucchini (courgettes), sliced diagonally
- 500 g (1 lb) tomatoes, thickly sliced
- 3 green capsicums (peppers), cored, seeded and sliced
- freshly ground black pepper

Cut eggplants (aubergines) into 1 cm (½ in) slices. Sprinkle with salt and leave for 30 minutes. Rinse and pat dry.

Heat half the oil in a heavy-based pan, add onions and garlic and gently fry until onion is soft. Add eggplant (aubergine) and fry for 5 minutes, stirring frequently. Remove eggplant (aubergine) from pan, add zucchini (courgette) and gently fry until soft, adding extra oil if necessary. Return the fried eggplant (aubergine) to the pan. Add the tomatoes and capsicum (pepper) and season with pepper. Cover and simmer for 30 to 40 minutes or until the ratatouille is very soft.

Serve warm or chilled, as an entrée or as a salad accompaniment to lamb or beef.

SERVES 12

SALAD NICOISE

A typically French salad from Nice, made with a combination of garden fresh ingredients and tuna.

- 1 small cos lettuce
- 1 green mignonette lettuce
- 250 g (8 oz) green beans, sliced
- 1 small white onion, thinly sliced
- 1 Lebanese cucumber, sliced
- 2 tablespoons capers
- 420 g (13 oz) can tuna in olive oil, drained
- 2 hard-boiled eggs, cut into quarters
- 4 vine-ripened tomatoes, cut into wedges
- 4 anchovy fillets, cut into fine strips

DRESSING

- 1 tablespoon tarragon-flavoured wine or balsamic vinegar
- 3 tablespoons olive oil
- 1 clove garlic, crushed
- ¼ teaspoon freshly ground black pepper
- 1 tablespoon finely chopped fresh parsley (optional)

Wash lettuce well in cold water and separate the leaves. Drain and shake dry in a clean tea towel. Cover and refrigerate for 10 minutes.

Lightly cook beans in a steamer or a microwave oven, then refresh in iced water. Drain well.

Tear lettuce and place pieces in a salad bowl. Arrange the remaining salad ingredients on top in given order.

To Prepare Dressing: Combine the dressing ingredients in a screw-top jar and shake until blended.

Just before serving, sprinkle the dressing over the salad and toss gently to combine at the table.

Serve accompanied by buttered new potatoes (chats) or warm French bread.

SERVES 4

PASTA SALAD WITH PESTO DRESSING

Pesto is an Italian sauce made with basil and Parmesan cheese. Once made, the dressing can be kept refrigerated for up to 3 months. Use to add extra flavour to pasta, soup, vegetables, poached fish or baby new potatoes.

250 g (8 oz) green tagliatelle or
fettucine noodles

1 cup baby spinach leaves

1 punnet cherry or tear drop
tomatoes

4 thick slices cooked leg ham,
diced

PESTO DRESSING

1 clove garlic, crushed

½ cup finely chopped fresh basil

3 tablespoons grated Parmesan
cheese

30 g (1 oz) ground pine nuts or
walnuts

4 tablespoons virgin olive oil

3 tablespoons balsamic vinegar

Cook pasta in 2 litres (64 fl oz) of boiling salted water for 10 to 12 minutes, until the pasta is *al dente*. Adding 1 tablespoon of oil to the water will prevent the pasta sticking or boiling over. Drain well, rinse in cold water and drain again. Cut into manageable lengths with kitchen scissors.

Place pasta in a salad bowl with the remaining salad ingredients.

To Prepare Pesto Dressing: Combine all the ingredients in a large screw-topped jar and shake well to combine or process in a food processor. Sprinkle over the pasta salad and toss just before serving. Serve with a green salad and Italian bread rolls.

SERVES 4

FARMHOUSE SALAD

Rub bread slices with cut garlic cloves before cutting into cubes and frying for garlic-flavoured croutons.

1 bunch curly endive or oak leaf
lettuce

1 radicchio lettuce

1 iceberg lettuce (crisphead),
outer leaves removed

3 bacon rashers, chopped, with
rind and bones removed

3 tablespoons pine nuts

2 cups garlic-flavoured fried
croutons

1 tablespoon finely chopped fresh
basil

4 tomatoes, cut into wedges,
or 1 punnet cherry tomatoes

1 tablespoon lemon juice

1 teaspoon apple cider vinegar

2 tablespoons virgin olive oil

Rinse the endive, radicchio and iceberg lettuce in cold water, drain well and chill covered until ready to use.

Tear the lettuce, endive and radicchio into bite-sized pieces and put into a salad bowl. Fry bacon until crisp, drain well on paper towels. Sprinkle the warm bacon, pine nuts, croutons and basil over the salad greens. Add the tomatoes and toss through until combined.

Sprinkle the salad with lemon juice, vinegar and the olive oil just before serving.

Serve salad for a light lunch, perhaps with coddled (lightly boiled) eggs.

SERVES 6

GREEK SALAD

1 butterleaf lettuce

4 vine-ripened tomatoes, cut into
wedges, or 1 punnet cherry
tomatoes

4 shallots (spring onions), thinly
sliced

1 white onion, thinly sliced

2 sticks celery, sliced

1 green capsicum (pepper),
seeded and sliced

12 large black olives

250 g (8 oz) feta cheese, cut
into cubes

DRESSING

3 tablespoons olive oil

1 tablespoon lemon juice

1 tablespoon chopped fresh
oregano or pinch dried oregano

pinch of salt

freshly ground black pepper

Wash the lettuce, drain and dry carefully and tear into bite-sized pieces. Place lettuce with the remaining ingredients in a salad bowl and toss gently.

To Prepare Dressing: Combine all the dressing ingredients in a screw-topped jar and shake until well blended. Just before serving, sprinkle over the salad.

Serve salad accompanied by wedges of olive bread or herb flavoured bread.

SERVES 6

TOMATOES
VINAIGRETTE

- *1 kg (2 lb) ripe tomatoes*
- *4 shallots (spring onions), sliced*
- *½ cup shredded fresh basil*
- *4 tablespoons olive oil*
- *4 tablespoons red wine or balsamic vinegar*
- *1 clove garlic, crushed*
- *2 tablespoons chopped capers*
- *2 tablespoons chopped gherkin*
- *salt*
- *freshly ground black pepper*

Wash and dry tomatoes and slice thickly. Layer tomatoes in a shallow bowl, sprinkling shallots and basil over each layer. Mix all remaining ingredients together and pour over tomatoes. Cover and marinate for at least 1 hour before serving.

SERVES 8

Tomatoes Vinaigrette

TOMATO CITRUS SALAD

Serve this tangy salad as an accompaniment to cold ham or poultry or poached salmon. Vine-ripened tomatoes will make a well flavoured salad.

1 kg (2 lb) tomatoes, cored, peeled and thickly sliced

8 tear drop tomatoes, halved

1 teaspoon caster sugar

salt and freshly ground black pepper

4 navel or other seedless oranges

4 tablespoons French Dressing (see recipe page 57)

4 tablespoons sliced sun-dried tomatoes

1 tablespoon snipped chives, to garnish

Sprinkle tomatoes with the sugar and season with salt and pepper. Carefully remove rind from one orange and cut the rind into julienne strips. Blanch the strips in boiling water for 3 to 4 minutes, then drain and refresh with cold water. Set aside. Peel the other oranges with a serrated knife, removing all the pith, then cut them all into segments.

Arrange the tomato slices and orange segments on a serving dish and sprinkle the French Dressing over. Scatter sun-dried tomatoes over the top. Garnish with the strips of orange rind and snipped chives and serve chilled.

SERVES 8

TOMATO AND ONION SALAD

A colourful and refreshing salad that's popular for summer barbecues.

6 ripe tomatoes, cored

1 large purple or Spanish onion, thinly sliced

4 tablespoons French Dressing (see recipe page 57)

2 teaspoons wholegrain mustard

2 tablespoons chopped fresh parsley

1 tablespoon snipped chives

Thinly slice the tomatoes and arrange on a flat plate. Push out the onion rings and arrange over the tomatoes.

Whisk the dressing, mustard and parsley together and pour over the tomatoes. Cover and chill until serving time.

Serve sprinkled with chives. This is a good salad to serve as part of a barbecue meal or with barbecued chicken and wholemeal bread rolls.

SERVES 4 TO 6

FRENCH DRESSING

French Dressing is a must with green salad vegetables and many other salads. This recipe is the basis of many fine salad dressings that add pizzazz to leafy green vegetables. To vary the flavour or add a gourmet touch, use the unique flavours of walnut, almond, macadamia or rape seed oil blended with a little balsamic, herb or strawberry-flavoured wine vinegar. These are all quite strong, so measure carefully and combine with virgin or standard olive oil or polyunsaturated vegetable oil to make up the correct proportions.

2 tablespoons white wine vinegar

¼ teaspoon salt

12 to 16 grinds freshly ground black pepper

½ teaspoon caster sugar

½ teaspoon mustard powder

2 plump cloves garlic, peeled and crushed (optional)

½ cup (125 ml/4 fl oz) olive oil

Combine vinegar, salt and pepper, sugar, mustard and garlic in a screw-topped jar. Shake until well blended. Add the oil and shake well until combined.

Store in the refrigerator until required. The dressing will keep for several weeks stored in this manner. Use as required to dress salads. If the oil solidifies, stand at room temperature to allow it to soften, then shake well before use.

MAKES ¾ CUP (185 ML/6 FL OZ)

TO STERILISE BOTTLES AND JARS FOR DRESSINGS YOU WISH TO STORE

To sterilise bottles and jars, first wash them in hot soapy water. Rinse with boiling water then turn the jars upside down on a clean dry tea towel. Using tongs, place the jars on a baking tray. Place in the oven at 150°C (300°F) for 15 minutes.

Tomato Coolers – Refreshing Drinks for Summertime

Long, hot summer days are perfect for sitting under a tree
with a good book and a long cool drink.
These drinks are refreshing as well as being vitamin enriched. We have
included both alcoholic and non-alcoholic drinks.
Make up a large jug, pop it in the refrigerator and you will have a great
pick-me-up ready and waiting.
The Herbed Tomato Juice is a wonderful way to start the day and
the Sherried Tomato Juice is a great way to end the day.
A tomato juice drink makes a wonderful addition to the buffet table. It will
be colourful and offers guests a healthy alternative.
We have outlined a few recipes below but there are many variations you
could try. Don't be afraid to pop your favourite flavours together in
the blender and create your own signature drink.

TOMATO REFRESHER

- 3 large ripe tomatoes, cored, peeled and chopped
- 1 cucumber, peeled, seeded and chopped
- 1 stick celery, chopped
- salt and pepper

Combine all the ingredients in an electric blender or food processor and process until smooth. Pour into a glass jug, cover and chill in refrigerator. Serve cold with ice cubes.

MAKES APPROXIMATELY 3 CUPS (750 ML/24 FL OZ)

YOGHURT TOMATO MIX

- 250 g (8 oz) ripe tomatoes, cored, peeled and chopped
- 200 g (6½ oz) natural yoghurt
- 2 teaspoons chilli sauce
- ¼ teaspoon lemon juice
- paprika
- mint leaves, to garnish

Purée the tomatoes in a food processor or blender. Mix in the yoghurt, chilli sauce and lemon juice, then season with a dash of paprika. Chill thoroughly and serve garnished with mint leaves.

MAKES APPROXIMATELY 2 CUPS (500 ML/16 FL OZ)

ZESTY BLOODY MARY

- 2⅓ cups (600 ml/20 fl oz) tomato juice
- 1¼ cups (300 ml/10 fl oz) vodka
- 1½ teaspoons Worcestershire sauce
- ½ teaspoon chilli or Tabasco sauce
- ¾ teaspoon celery salt (optional)
- juice of 3 limes or 1½ lemons

Mix all the ingredients together, then pour over ice cubes into tall glasses.

MAKES 3⅔ CUPS (900 ML/30 FL OZ)

HERBED TOMATO JUICE

Served at breakfast, this juice will provide the necessary energy to start the day.

1.5 kg (3 lb) ripe tomatoes
½ cup (125 ml/4 fl oz) water
1 onion, sliced
1 stick celery, sliced
4 sprigs fresh basil
3 sprigs fresh parsley
1 bay leaf
salt
paprika
dash Worcestershire sauce
lemon juice

Core tomatoes and cut into quarters. Put tomatoes into a pan with the water, onion, celery and herbs. Simmer covered, until the tomatoes have broken up. Strain through a sieve, pressing pulp through with a wooden spoon, to form a purée. Season to taste with salt, paprika, Worcestershire sauce and a dash of lemon juice. Pour into a glass jug or jar, cover and chill before serving.

MAKES APPROXIMATELY 4 CUPS (1 LITRE/32 FL OZ)

TOMATO PUNCH

As a healthy, non-alcoholic alternative to punch try using one of these tomato drinks. Float lemon slices, celery or cucumber slices and herbs in the bowl for a colourful effect.
On a really hot summer day, chill the glasses as well as the bowl or jug to ensure a totally refreshing drink.

MINTED TOMATO JUICE

2 cups (500 ml/16 fl oz) tomato juice
rind and juice of ½ lemon
1 teaspoon white wine or apple cider vinegar
1 teaspoon finely chopped mint
salt, pepper and nutmeg

Combine all the ingredients and chill thoroughly. Remove the lemon rind before serving.

MAKES 2 CUPS (500 ML/16 FL OZ)

SHERRIED TOMATO JUICE

¾ cup (180 ml/6 fl oz) tomato juice
salt
pepper
dash Tabasco sauce
1 teaspoon dry sherry
Worcestershire sauce
lemon wedge, to garnish

Chill the tomato juice, then season with the salt, pepper and Tabasco sauce. Just before serving, stir in the sherry and a few drops of Worcestershire sauce to taste. Garnish with a thin wedge of lemon.

MAKES 1 CUP (250 ML/8 FL OZ)

GARNISHES FOR TOMATO COOLERS

CUCUMBER SWIRL

Peal thin strips from a cucumber so that you achieve a green and white striped effect. Slice thinly, make a slit from the edge to the middle and place on the side of the glass.

ICE CUBE SURPRISE

Place mint leaves, small slices of lemon or herbs into an ice cube tray. Fill with water and freeze so that the leaves or fruit are suspended in the ice. Use in drinks as a colourful garnish.

CITRUS SWIRLS

Slice lemons or limes thinly. Remove any pips. Cut halfway through the circle and place on the side of the glass.

EDIBLE BLOOMS

Cucumber and zucchini both have edible flowers. If you grow your own, pick the flowers, wash gently and use to garnish drinks and bowls.

Snacks and Finger Food

*T*omatoes are ideal for tasty snacks, delicious finger food for parties, for 'grazing on' and also for light meals. Use them in dips, slice them for sensational sandwiches, chop them and cook them or stuff them. These tomato snacks are quick and simple to prepare and light and tasty to eat.

TOMATOES AND SALMON ON RYE

2 slices rye bread

mayonnaise

2 vine-ripened tomatoes

1 tablespoon fresh basil leaves, torn

100 g (3½ oz) thinly sliced smoked salmon

bean sprouts

1 tablespoon French Dressing or Tomato Flavoured Oil (see recipes pages 57 and 86)

Spread rye bread with mayonnaise, slice tomatoes and arrange, overlapping, over mayonnaise. Sprinkle basil leaves over tomatoes. Roll salmon slices up neatly and place attractively on top of tomatoes and basil. Sprinkle bean sprouts generously over the top and drizzle with dressing.

Serve immediately.

SERVES 2

HOT TURKEY AND TOMATO MELTS

125 g (4 oz) cheddar cheese, grated

2 teaspoons wholegrain mustard

2 tablespoons milk or light sour cream

2 to 3 drops Tabasco sauce

4 slices wholemeal (wholegrain) bread

4 thick slices white turkey meat

4 large slices tomato

4 bacon rashers, partially cooked, rind removed

2 tablespoons grated Parmesan cheese

Mix grated cheddar cheese with mustard and milk. Season with Tabasco sauce.

Toast the bread on one side only, then top the untoasted side with turkey, tomato, cheese mixture and bacon.

Sprinkle the Parmesan cheese over and grill until the cheese mixture is brown and bubbling. Serve hot for a light lunch or supper, accompanied by tossed salad greens.

Variations: Cooked ham, chicken or sliced salami may be substituted for the turkey.

SERVES 4

YOGHURT TOMATO DIP WITH PAKORAS

A delicious, healthy entrée. The vegetable shapes by themselves are attractive, and they are enhanced by the tangy tomato dip.

TOMATO DIP

1 cup (250 ml/8 fl oz) fresh Tomato Purée (see recipe page 86)

1¼ cups (300 ml/10 fl oz) natural yoghurt

salt and pepper

1 teaspoon ground cumin

1 tablespoon chopped fresh coriander, to garnish

BATTER

125 g (4 oz) chick pea flour

salt and pepper

1 teaspoon chilli powder

1 teaspoon ground cumin

1 teaspoon ground turmeric

about 200 ml (6½ fl oz) water, to mix

VEGETABLES

1 potato, peeled and cut into thick chips

1 carrot, peeled and cut into thick chips

1 small eggplant (aubergine), cut into 2 cm (¾ in) cubes

1 green capsicum (pepper), seeded and cut into squares

250 g (8 oz) cauliflower florets

3 cups (750 ml/24 fl oz) oil, for frying

To Prepare Tomato Dip: Combine the tomato purée, yoghurt, salt, pepper, and cumin. Just before serving, garnish with the coriander.

To Prepare Batter: Combine the flour, salt and pepper, chilli powder, cumin and turmeric, then gradually whisk in enough water to form a smooth batter.

Prepare vegetables as directed. Heat the oil in a deep fryer or large pan. Dip the vegetables into the batter, then deep fry in small batches until golden brown. Drain on paper towels.

Serve the Pakoras on a plate with the Tomato Dip as a party savoury or as part of an Indian meal.

SERVES 6

Pictured on previous pages: Thai Tomato Dip with Crudités, Sun-dried Tomato Pâté Crostini (page 68)

HUMMUS-STUFFED CHERRY TOMATOES

1 cup chick peas, soaked overnight

2 cloves garlic, halved

½ cup (125 ml/4 fl oz) tahini

3 tablespoons lemon juice

salt

cayenne pepper

paprika

1 punnet cherry tomatoes

1 teaspoon olive oil

Rinse the chick peas and put in a saucepan with 1½ cups (375 ml/ 12 fl oz) water (enough to cover). Bring to the boil, reduce the heat and simmer for 1 hour until tender. Drain, and reserve the liquid. Reserve ¼ cup chick peas for the garnish. Purée the chick peas with the garlic in a food processor or blender. Blend in the tahini and lemon juice, then add a little of the reserved cooking liquid to make a thick, piping consistency. Season with the salt, cayenne pepper and paprika. Chill the hummus, covered with plastic wrap, for 2 hours.

Wash and dry the cherry tomatoes, slice tops off, then scoop out seeds and pulp (use in a juice or sauce). Pipe the hummus into each tomato shell and drizzle a few drops of oil over the top. Garnish with the reserved chick peas. Serve as party finger food.

Note: This dish may be prepared ahead and stored, covered, in the refrigerator for 3 hours.

MAKES ABOUT 30

SUN-DRIED TOMATO PIKELETS

750 g (1½ lb) tomatoes, cored, peeled and chopped

4 eggs

125 g (4 oz) self-raising flour

125 g (4 oz) dried breadcrumbs

60 g (2 oz) butter or margarine, melted

1 tablespoon finely chopped parsley

2 tablespoons finely chopped sun-dried tomatoes

salt and pepper

Put tomatoes into a heavy-based pan and simmer over low heat until pulpy. (This can also be done in a microwave-safe bowl in a microwave oven. Cover and cook on High for 5 minutes.) Set aside and cool.

Beat the eggs, then stir in the sifted flour, breadcrumbs, butter, parsley and sun-dried tomatoes. Season with salt and pepper. Add tomatoes to the egg mixture, stirring until well blended.

Drop the mixture, a tablespoon at a time, into a hot, greased frying pan. Cook for 1 to 2 minutes, or until browned on the bottom, then turn over and brown on the other side.

Serve immediately, for breakfast, brunch or just a tasty snack.

SERVES 4

SAVOURY TOMATO CASES

3 rashers bacon, chopped with rind and bones removed

1 onion, finely chopped

1 large tomato, cored, seeded and chopped

170 g (5½ oz) corn kernels

freshly ground black pepper

pinch sugar

1 tablespoon shredded fresh basil

10 to 12 small savoury pastry cases (vol-au-vents) or breadcases, for serving

thinly sliced cherry tomatoes and finely sliced black olives to garnish

Preheat oven to 180°C (350°F).

Cook the bacon in its own fat until crisp, then transfer it to paper towels to drain. Cook the onion in the bacon fat for 3 minutes, or until soft. Add the tomato and corn and cook together until tender. Season with pepper and a pinch of sugar, then stir in the bacon and basil.

Fill the prepared cases with the filling and bake for 10 minutes, or until heated through.

Serve warm, as party finger food, garnished with cherry tomatoes and slivers of black olives.

MAKES 10 TO 12

CHICKEN LIVER SNACK

Chicken livers are nourishing, easy to prepare and taste tender and delicious if handled correctly. Always rinse livers with cold water, cut into lobes and remove any tubes with kitchen scissors. Discard any livers that are slightly green, as these are very bitter to eat.

30 g (1 oz) butter or margarine

1 small onion, finely chopped

1 tomato, cored and chopped

4 mushrooms, chopped

salt and pepper

125 g (4 oz) chicken livers, cleaned and chopped

1 tablespoon chopped fresh herbs

Melt butter in a frying pan and gently fry the onion for 5 minutes or until soft but not browned. Add the tomato and mushrooms and season with salt and pepper. Cook for 3 minutes, then push the vegetables to one side. Add the chicken livers and herbs and fry gently for 4 minutes or until cooked, stirring occasionally.

Serve over cooked rice or spaghetti, or on wholemeal toast.

SERVES 1 TO 2

BASIL BUTTER

Basil Butter can be frozen. Keep some handy for sandwiches, topping grilled tomatoes and barbecued fish, for herb bread and jacket-baked potatoes.

90 g (3 oz) butter, softened

1 clove garlic, crushed

2 tablespoons chopped fresh basil

1 tablespoon chopped fresh parsley

good squeeze lemon juice

salt and pepper

Beat butter until soft, add remaining ingredients and season with salt and pepper. Stir well, until the ingredients are thoroughly blended, then turn onto a piece of aluminium foil and form into a log shape. Seal well and freeze until firm. Store in refrigerator or freezer.

Place the freshly creamed Basil Butter onto a sheet of aluminium foil.

Using a metal spatula, roll the butter into a log shape, wrapping the aluminium foil around it.

Twist the ends tightly to seal and freeze until firm.

OPEN SANDWICHES

Open sandwiches are an ideal snack solution: they are healthy and quick to prepare. Why cover colourful, fresh ingredients with a second slice of bread when they can be served in delicious Danish style?

BREAD SUGGESTIONS

The following breads make delicious bases for open sandwiches, with flavour, texture and fibre adding considerably to the sandwiches' appeal. These breads will stay fresher for longer.

- Pumpernickel
- Rye
- Sweet and Sour Latvian
- Schinkenbrot
- Barley and Sunflower
- Wholegrain

SUGGESTED TOPPINGS

- Basil Butter (see recipe page 64), sliced vine-ripened tomato, finely chopped shallots and strips of prosciutto

- lettuce, halved cherry tomatoes, tuna, finely sliced red onion and mayonnaise

- sliced ham, sliced vine-ripened tomato, Swiss cheese, chives and pecans

- ricotta cheese, tomato wedges topped with strips of smoked turkey breast and mustard cress or bean sprouts

- wedges of Camembert or Brie cheese, yellow tear drop tomatoes, sun-dried tomatoes in oil and snow pea sprouts

Open Sandwiches

RED PEPPER AND TOMATO OMELETTE

2 red capsicums (peppers), seeded and cut into thin strips

30 g (1 oz) butter

1 small onion, chopped

2 cloves garlic, crushed

2 tomatoes, cored and chopped

4 eggs

2 teaspoons chopped fresh oregano

salt and pepper

Blanch the capsicums (peppers) in boiling salted water for 2 minutes, then drain. Heat butter in a large omelette pan and fry the onion and garlic until soft but not browned. Add the capsicum (pepper) and tomato and cook for a further 5 to 10 minutes, until vegetables are tender.

Beat the eggs and season with oregano, salt and pepper. Pour egg mixture over vegetables, tilting the pan to spread the omelette evenly. Cook over medium heat, stirring with a fork, until the eggs have just set. Then place the pan under a hot grill for 1 to 2 minutes, or until top is golden and has set.

Serve immediately, accompanied by a green salad.

SERVES 2

TOMATO OMELETTE

60 g (2 oz) butter or margarine

1 small onion, finely chopped

500 g (1 lb) tomatoes, cored and chopped

salt and pepper

2 tablespoons chopped fresh parsley

8 eggs

Melt half the butter in a pan, add the onion and fry gently for a few minutes. Add tomatoes and season with salt and pepper. Cook uncovered for 30 minutes, or until mixture has thickened. Stir in parsley.

Break 2 eggs into a bowl and whisk until thoroughly combined.

Melt a knob of the remaining butter in an omelette pan until foaming but not brown. Add the beaten eggs and cook over medium heat, moving the mixture with a fork until lightly set. Loosen the omelette with a palette knife then fold the omelette in half. Spoon one-quarter of the tomato mixture over the centre and slide from the pan onto a dinner plate.

Make three more omelettes in the same way. Serve with a green salad.

SERVES 4

FRIED GREEN TOMATOES

This American dish is delicious with grilled bacon or sausages for breakfast or lunch.

4 green tomatoes

1 egg, beaten

2 tablespoons milk

60 g (2 oz) plain flour

250 g (8 oz) cornmeal

vegetable oil

Cut tomatoes across into 4 slices. Beat egg with milk. Dip the tomato slices into the flour and coat both sides, then dip them into the egg mixture, brushing all over. Finally, dip them into the cornmeal (on a sheet of greaseproof paper). Flick cornmeal over tomato slices until well coated and shake off excess.

Heat sufficient oil in a large frying pan to cover base generously. Fry tomatoes until golden underneath then turn over and fry other side until golden. Drain well.

Serve for a snack or for breakfast with bacon or bratwurst sausages.

SERVES 4 TO 8, ACCORDING TO APPETITE!

Red Pepper and Tomato Omelette (front), Tomato Omelette (back)

SUN-DRIED TOMATO PATE CROSTINI

Pictured on pages 60-61.

1 French loaf

olive oil

1 jar tomato pâté

250 g (8 oz) cottage or ricotta cheese

250 g (8 oz) jar sun-dried tomatoes in oil, drained

cherry tomatoes and basil, to garnish

Preheat oven to 180°C (350°F).

Cut loaf diagonally into 1.5 cm (½ in) slices. Place slices on a baking tray and brush with olive oil. Bake for 5 minutes or until crisp. Allow to cool.

Spread crostini with tomato pâté then top with some cottage cheese. Slice sun-dried tomatoes into strips and sprinkle on top of cottage cheese.

Serve Tomato Pâté Crostini as a party savoury or finger food snack, on a platter garnished with cherry tomatoes and basil.

MAKES ABOUT 24

THAI TOMATO DIP WITH CRUDITES

Pictured on pages 60-61.

THAI TOMATO DIP

3 tablespoons mayonnaise

300 ml (10 fl oz) light sour cream

2 tablespoons natural yoghurt

3 tablespoons tomato paste

3 tablespoons tomato chutney

1 clove garlic, crushed

1 teaspoon finely chopped ginger

1 tablespoon finely chopped lemon grass

finely grated rind of 1 lime

2 tablespoons chopped coriander

CRUDITES

2 carrots, peeled

3 sticks celery

4 zucchini (courgettes)

250 g (8 oz) broccoli, broken into florets

250 g (8 oz) cherry or tear drop tomatoes

125 g (4 oz) button mushrooms

To Prepare Thai Tomato Dip: Combine the ingredients, folding together until well blended. Spoon into a serving dish, cover and chill until serving time.

To Prepare Crudités: Cut the carrots, celery and zucchini into match-stick lengths. Rinse the broccoli and tomatoes in cold water and dry well. Brush mushrooms clean with a pastry brush.

To Serve: Place the dip in the centre of a platter, surrounded by the vegetables. Serve as party finger food.

SERVES 6

TOMATO AND AVOCADO FOCACCIA

4 portions focaccia, each cut 15 cm x 10 cm (6 in x 4 in)

olive oil with crushed garlic

tapenade or olive pâté

4 vine-ripened tomatoes

1 avocado

250 g (8 oz) round Camembert or Brie cheese

2 cups salad greens or snow pea sprouts

2 tablespoons French Dressing (see recipe page 57)

Slice focaccia in half through the centre. Brush cut surfaces with olive oil and crushed garlic. Place, oiled side up, under a hot grill and toast lightly.

Spread grilled side of bottom halves with tapenade. Slice tomatoes and place on top of tapenade. Cut avocado in half, remove stone, then cut into quarters and remove skin. Slice avocado and place on top of tomatoes. Cut cheese into wedges and place on top of avocado. Top each layered focaccia with ½ cup salad greens and sprinkle French Dressing over each.

Place top of focaccia on top at an angle and serve immediately.

SERVES 4

Tomato and Avocado Focaccia

CHEESE SOUFFLE IN TOMATOES

8 medium-sized tomatoes

40 g (1⅓ oz) butter or margarine

1 tablespoon plain flour

½ cup (125 ml/4 fl oz) milk

salt and pepper

125 g (4 oz) tasty cheese, grated

3 eggs, separated

Preheat oven to 180°C (350°F).

Slice the tops off tomatoes, scoop out the seeds and fleshy membranes and set aside.

Melt butter in a saucepan and add the flour, salt and pepper. Cook for 1 minute over medium heat, stirring continuously. Add milk and tomato flesh and bring to the boil. Stir in the cheese until well blended. Remove from heat and mix in the egg yolks.

Whisk egg whites until stiff peaks form, then fold gently into the mixture. Spoon soufflé into the tomato shells until each one is three-quarters full. Arrange in a greased shallow ovenproof dish and bake for 15 minutes.

Serve immediately, with new potatoes and salad, for a light meal.

SERVES 4

CAULIFLOWER AND TOMATO GRATIN

1 small cauliflower, cut into florets

500 g (1 lb) tomatoes, cored and roughly chopped

salt and pepper

60 g (2 oz) butter or margarine

4 tablespoons plain flour

2 cups (500 ml/16 fl oz) milk

60 g (2 oz) Cheddar cheese, grated

30 g (1 oz) fresh breadcrumbs

60 g (2 oz) Parmesan cheese, grated

Preheat oven to 190°C (375°F).

Cook cauliflower in boiling salted water or in a microwave oven until tender, then drain and refresh under cold running water.

Place the cauliflower and tomatoes in a greased ovenproof serving dish and season with salt and pepper. Melt butter in a saucepan, add flour and stir over a medium heat for 1 to 2 minutes. Add milk and bring to the boil, stirring continuously. Stir in Cheddar cheese until melted. Pour sauce over the cauliflower and tomatoes. Combine the breadcrumbs and Parmesan cheese and sprinkle over the sauce.

Bake for 15 to 20 minutes, or until bubbling hot.

Serve with wholemeal toast, for a light meal.

SERVES 4 TO 6

RICE AND TOMATO PILAF

30 g (1 oz) butter or margarine

1 onion, finely chopped

2 tomatoes, cored and chopped

2½ cups (625 ml/20 fl oz) chicken or vegetable stock

3 tablespoons tomato paste

250 g (8 oz) long grain rice, rinsed

1½ tablespoons oil

3 tablespoons white wine vinegar

freshly ground black pepper

2 tablespoons sun-dried tomatoes in oil, drained and chopped

Melt butter in a large heavy-based pan and cook onion gently until transparent. Add tomatoes and bring to the boil. Add chicken stock and return to the boil. Stir in the tomato paste, rice, oil, vinegar and pepper and continue to boil until excess liquid has evaporated. Reduce heat, cover pan and simmer for 7 minutes, or until rice is tender. Stir in the sun-dried tomatoes before serving.

Serve Rice and Tomato Pilaf with barbecued chicken or grilled prawns.

SERVES 4 TO 6

SIMMERING FOOD

When simmering ensure that you have a very gentle heat. Too high a temperature can cause food to stick to the bottom of the pan and burn. Simmer rings are available for use on gas stoves. They provide a filter between the heat and the pan.

MIDDLE EASTERN TOMATOES

- 8 large tomatoes
- 4 tablespoons olive oil
- 2 onions, finely chopped
- 165 g (5½ oz) long grain rice
- 2 tablespoons currants
- 2 tablespoons pine nuts
- 2 tablespoons finely chopped mint
- 2 tablespoons finely chopped parsley
- salt and pepper
- 1¼ cups (300 ml/10 fl oz) water or vegetable stock
- juice of 2 lemons

Preheat oven to 180°C (350°F).

Slice the tops off the tomatoes and scoop out the seeds and fleshy membranes, reserving tomato tops, pulp and seeds. Heat oil in a pan and gently fry onions until golden brown. Stir in tomato pulp, then mix in rice, currants, pine nuts and herbs. Simmer for 2 minutes, then add water and cook slowly for 10 minutes, or until rice begins to soften. Season to taste.

Spoon mixture into the tomato shells, allowing room at the top for the rice to swell. Replace tops and brush all over with extra oil. Arrange in an oiled baking dish, pour lemon juice around tomatoes and cook for 35 to 40 minutes.

Serve Middle Eastern Tomatoes with warm pitta or Turkish bread.

SERVES 4

SPINACH-STUFFED TOMATOES

- 4 to 6 large tomatoes
- 30 g (1 oz) butter or margarine
- 1 onion, finely chopped
- 500 g (1 lb) spinach, chopped, cooked, and well drained
- 1 tablespoon sweet chilli sauce
- 2 teaspoons chopped fresh thyme
- 30 g (1 oz) fresh breadcrumbs
- 2 eggs, beaten
- 60 g (2 oz) grated Parmesan cheese
- 30 g (1 oz) extra butter or margarine

Preheat oven to 180°F (350°C).

Slice the tops off the tomatoes, scoop out seeds and fleshy membrane and set aside.

Heat butter in a pan and gently fry onion until soft but not browned. Add spinach, chilli sauce, thyme and breadcrumbs, mix in eggs and cook, stirring constantly, until well combined.

Spoon mixture into tomato shells, sprinkle with grated cheese and dot with additional butter. Bake for 15 minutes, or until brown on top and heated through.

Serve hot, for brunch, with fried bacon, gammon rashers or thin pork sausages.

SERVES 4 TO 6

CHICKEN AND TOMATO CROISSANTS

Croissants are readily available both fresh and frozen. Keep some on hand to create easy snacks.

- 4 shallots (spring onions), sliced
- 8 thin slices rolled chicken breast, cut into strips
- 1 stick celery, chopped
- 2 tomatoes, chopped
- 60 g (2 oz) mushrooms, sliced
- salt and pepper
- tomato chutney (see recipe page 87)
- 4 croissants
- fresh herbs, to garnish

Preheat oven to 190°C (375°F).

Mix sliced shallots with chicken, celery, tomatoes and mushrooms. Add salt and pepper.

Heat croissants in oven for 5 minutes. Slice them and put the bases onto individual serving plates. Spoon chicken mixture over and top with chutney and the remaining croissant half.

Serve croissants hot, garnished with herbs and accompanied by a side salad.

SERVES 4

Tomato Classics

These delicious traditional recipes that remain favourites would not be possible without the rich colour and tangy flavour of the tomato. With meat, chicken, fish and vegetables, tomatoes give us Cacciatore, Chasseur, Parmigiana, Marengo and many other colourful classics.

CRAYFISH WITH TOMATO AND WINE

1 x 2 kg (4 lb) live crayfish

salt and cayenne pepper

30 g (1 oz) butter

1 tablespoon oil

1 onion, finely chopped

4 shallots (spring onions), sliced

3 tablespoons brandy

3 tablespoons white wine

3 tablespoons fish stock

3 tomatoes, peeled, seeded and chopped

1 teaspoon tomato paste

30 g (1 oz) butter, extra

fresh herbs, to garnish

Ask the fishmonger to kill the crayfish. Split crayfish in half lengthwise, cut off the head section and remove and reserve any roe. Twist off legs and cut tail section into thick slices. Season tail pieces with salt and cayenne pepper.

Heat butter and oil in a frying pan. Add crayfish pieces, legs and onion and cook over gentle heat for 4 minutes. Add shallots and cook for a minute more. Pour in the heated brandy and flame. Shake the pan until the flames die down. Stir in remaining ingredients except for extra butter and herbs. Bring to the boil, reduce heat and simmer for 15 minutes, stirring occasionally.

Remove crayfish and keep warm on a serving dish.

Simmer sauce to thicken slightly, then stir through the roe and butter. Push through a sieve or purée in a food processor or blender. Taste, adjust seasonings, then reheat.

Coat crayfish with sauce and serve accompanied by rice.

SERVES 2

Crayfish with Tomato and Wine

ITALIAN STUFFED MUSSELS

Italian Stuffed Mussels

1 kg (2¼ lb) mussels (in shell), scrubbed, beards removed

2 tablespoons olive oil

1 onion, finely chopped

1 red capsicum (pepper), seeded and chopped

1 green capsicum (pepper), seeded and chopped

1 yellow capsicum (pepper), seeded and chopped

2 cloves garlic, crushed

50 g (2 oz) smoked prosciutto ham, finely chopped

425 g (13 oz) can tomatoes, drained and chopped

pinch saffron threads, soaked in 3 tablespoons dry white wine

salt and pepper

parsley sprigs, to garnish

Place mussels in a large pan and half fill with water. Cover, bring slowly to the boil and cook for 3 to 4 minutes. Drain, reserving 1 cup (250 ml/8 fl oz) liquid. Discard any unopened mussels.

Remove the top shell, loosen the mussel in the bottom shell. Heat the oil in a pan and gently fry onion and capsicum until softened but not browned. Add garlic and ham, then stir in the tomatoes and cook until the mixture thickens. Pour in the saffron liquid and strained reserved mussel liquid. Simmer until the mixture is thick and the liquid has almost evaporated, then season and cool. Top the mussels with the sauce and serve the shells on a platter garnished with parsley.

SERVES 6 FOR AN ENTREE

Pictured on previous pages: Chicken Chasseur (page 79), Lamb Noisettes Italian Style (page 83)

VEAL PARMIGIANA

Pounding the veal steaks before cooking will make them tender. Place veal between two sheets of plastic wrap and pound with a rolling pin or meat mallet. Milk-fed veal, available from some butchers, is very tender.

125 g (4 oz) dried breadcrumbs

90 g (3 oz) grated Parmesan cheese

12 small thin slices veal steak (schnitzel/escalopes)

60 g (2 oz) plain flour, seasoned with salt and pepper

2 eggs, beaten

4 tablespoons olive oil

1 large onion, chopped

1 clove garlic, crushed

1 kg (2 lb) can tomatoes, drained

3 tablespoons tomato paste

1 tablespoon chopped fresh basil

2 teaspoons chopped fresh thyme

salt and pepper

30 g to 45 g (1 oz to 1½ oz) butter or margarine

250 g (8 oz) mozzarella cheese, sliced

Preheat oven to 170°C (340°F).

Mix breadcrumbs with one-third of the Parmesan cheese on a shallow plate. Dip veal into the seasoned flour, then into the beaten egg, then coat with crumb and cheese mixture. Stand until dry.

Heat half the oil in a pan and gently fry onion and garlic until soft but not brown. Add tomatoes, tomato paste, basil, thyme, salt and pepper, cover pan and simmer for 15 minutes.

Heat remaining oil and butter in another frying pan and brown veal on both sides, a few pieces at a time. Add extra oil or butter if required.

Veal Parmigiana

Spoon part of the sauce into a shallow baking dish then arrange alternate, overlapping slices of veal and cheese in the dish. Spoon over the remaining sauce and sprinkle with the remaining Parmesan cheese. Bake for 20 minutes.

Serve hot, with rice and a mixed green salad.

SERVES 6

CHICKEN CACCIATORE

Very ripe tomatoes make this a colourful special occasion dish.

- *1.5 kg (3 lb) chicken pieces*
- *4 tablespoons plain flour, seasoned with salt and pepper*
- *2 tablespoons olive oil*
- *1 onion, chopped*
- *1 clove garlic, crushed*
- *½ red capsicum (pepper), seeded and cut into 1 cm (½ in) strips*
- *2 teaspoons sugar*
- *500 g (1 lb) cooking tomatoes*
- *3 tablespoons tomato paste*
- *1 tablespoon chopped fresh basil or oregano*
- *½ cup (125 ml/4 fl oz) dry white wine*
- *10 black olives*
- *Italian (continental) parsley, chopped, to garnish*

Remove any chicken fat and excess skin where possible. Coat chicken pieces with seasoned flour, shaking off any excess.

Heat oil in a large frying pan or cast-iron casserole dish and fry the chicken pieces for a few minutes on each side. Remove from pan. Add a little extra oil if necessary, then gently fry onion, garlic and capsicum for 3 minutes. Stir in the remaining ingredients and return chicken pieces to pan. Cover, bring to the boil, reduce heat and simmer for 30 to 40 minutes, or until chicken is tender.

Adjust seasonings if necessary. Serve hot, sprinkled with parsley and accompanied by pasta.

SERVES 4

Chicken Cacciatore

BARBECUED PORK SPARE RIBS

2 tablespoons vegetable oil

2 cloves garlic, chopped

2 onions, finely chopped

¾ cup (185 ml/6 fl oz) Tomato Purée (see recipe page 86)

½ cup (125 ml/4 fl oz) vinegar

½ cup (125 ml/4 fl oz) honey

1 teaspoon mustard powder

2 tablespoons light soy sauce

1 cup (250 ml/8 fl oz) beef stock

2 kg (4 lb) pork spare ribs

finely sliced shallots (spring onions) to garnish

Preheat oven to 200°C to 230°C (400°F to 450°F).

Heat oil in a pan and gently fry garlic and onions until softened. Mix in the tomato purée, vinegar, honey, mustard, soy sauce and stock. Bring to the boil, then reduce heat and simmer for 15 minutes. Remove from heat.

Using a large, shallow dish, put the ribs into the cooked barbecue marinade and marinate for 30 minutes.

Place a wire rack in a roasting pan and arrange the ribs, fat-side up, on the rack. Brush the ribs liberally with the marinade. Roast in the oven for approximately 1 hour, basting the ribs every 15 minutes, or barbecue over medium heat, turning frequently.

When cooked, cut the ribs into individual portions to serve. Spoon remaining sauce over the top and sprinkle with finely sliced shallots (spring onions). Serve with rice and a crisp salad.

SERVES 4

Barbecued Pork Spare Ribs

CHICKEN CHASSEUR

Pictured on pages 72-73.

1.5 kg (3 lb) chicken or chicken pieces

60 g (2 oz) butter or margarine

2 tablespoons olive oil

salt and pepper

1 onion or 4 French shallots, chopped

125 g (4 oz) button mushrooms, sliced

3 tablespoons dry white wine

1¼ cups Tasty Tomato Sauce (see recipe page 19)

250 g (8 oz) tomatoes, cored, peeled and chopped

chopped parsley, to garnish

Cut legs off chicken and cut into two at the joint. Remove wishbone and wing tips, leaving two equal portions on the breast. Slice off the wings, then the breast and cut into two. Reserve carcass for stock.

Heat butter and oil in a large heavy-based pan. Season chicken with salt and pepper and add it to the pan in the following order: drumsticks, thighs, wings and breast. Cook until golden. Cover pan with a lid and cook for approximately 10 minutes, then transfer chicken pieces to a dish and keep them warm.

Add onion to pan and fry for 2 minutes. Stir in the mushrooms, cover pan and cook gently for 4 minutes. Drain off fat, add white wine and boil until reduced by half. Add the Tasty Tomato Sauce and chopped tomatoes, return chicken to pan and simmer for 15 minutes, or until chicken is tender. Adjust seasoning if necessary.

Serve Chicken Chasseur sprinkled with chopped parsley, accompanied by new potatoes or rice and a green vegetable.

SERVES 4

EASY LASAGNE

Most lasagne recipes are long and involved; layer upon layer of sauce, pasta and meat. Here is a recipe that is simple but not lacking in flavour.

500 g (1 lb) lasagne pasta, cooked

250 g (8 oz) cream cheese, softened

250 g (8 oz) cottage cheese

300 ml (10 fl oz) light sour cream

2 tablespoons olive oil

1 large onion, chopped

1 green capsicum (pepper), seeded and chopped

500 g (1 lb) beef, finely minced

salt and pepper

850 g (28 oz) can tomatoes, drained and chopped

300 g (10 oz) mushrooms, chopped

1 tablespoon chopped fresh basil

½ teaspoon sugar

185 g (6 oz) grated tasty cheese

Preheat oven to 180°C (350°F).

Drain the lasagne, rinse in warm water, then drain again on a clean tea towel. Arrange a layer of half the lasagne in a greased ovenproof dish approximately 17 cm x 25 cm (7 in x 10 in). Mix the cream cheese, cottage cheese and sour cream, and spread over the lasagne.

Heat oil in a frying pan and cook onion and capsicum until soft. Stir in the beef, salt and pepper and brown lightly. Drain off excess fat. Add tomatoes, mushrooms, basil and sugar. Cook for 20 minutes, or until thickened and well combined. Spoon mixture over the cheese mixture and top with more lasagne and the grated cheese. Bake for 30 to 40 minutes or until golden and bubbling.

Serve with green salad.

SERVES 6 TO 8

Trim fish tail and fins using kitchen scissors.

Spoon crab mixture into the cavity of the fish.

Pour the remaining Creole Sauce over the fish.

BAKED FISH SPANISH STYLE

Serve with crusty bread so that the sauce may be enjoyed to the fullest.

CREOLE SAUCE

20 g (⅔ oz) butter

1 tablespoon plain flour

1 cup (250 ml/8 fl oz) tomato juice

½ cup (125 ml/4 fl oz) dry white wine

1 small onion, finely chopped

1 tablespoon finely chopped parsley

1 small carrot, grated

1 clove garlic, crushed

½ red capsicum (pepper), seeded and finely chopped

½ green capsicum (pepper), seeded and finely chopped

pinch cayenne pepper

½ teaspoon salt

juice of 1 lemon, strained

1 stalk celery, finely chopped

250 g (8 oz) mushrooms, finely chopped

FISH

15 g (½ oz) butter

1 onion, finely chopped

1 green capsicum (pepper), seeded and finely chopped

400 g (13 oz) can crabmeat, drained and flaked

1 medium-sized snapper or large bream, cleaned and scaled

Preheat oven to 175°C (350°F).

To Prepare Creole Sauce: Melt butter in a saucepan, add flour, stir over medium heat for 1 minute. Gradually add tomato juice and wine, bring to the boil, stirring until smooth, then add the remaining ingredients. Simmer for 30 minutes. Cover and keep warm over very low heat while preparing the fish.

To Prepare Fish: Melt butter in a pan, add the onion and cook until softened, approximately 5 minutes. Add the capsicum and crabmeat, mixing well. Set aside until cool.

Trim the fish tail and fins using kitchen scissors. Season the cavity of the fish and spoon in the crab mixture. Secure the opening with skewers or toothpicks. Pour half the sauce into a greased baking dish large enough to hold the fish. Place the fish on the sauce and pour over the remaining sauce. Bake in the oven for 30 to 40 minutes or until the flesh flakes easily. Baste fish frequently with the sauce during baking.

Serve with rice and follow with a green salad.

SERVES 4

VEAL MARENGO

The Marengo was a dish created by Napoleon's French chef to mark the victory of the Battle of Marengo in 1800. The original recipe contained ingredients found close by the battlefield, including chicken and freshwater crayfish.

2 tablespoons olive oil

1 kg (2 lb) pie or stewing veal, cut into 2.5 cm (1 in) cubes

2 onions, finely chopped

1 tablespoon plain flour

2 tablespoons tomato paste

½ cup (125 ml/4 fl oz) white wine

1 cup (250 ml/8 fl oz) beef stock

2 cloves garlic, finely chopped

1 bouquet garni

250 g (8 oz) tomatoes, cored, peeled and chopped

salt

freshly ground black pepper

1 tablespoon chopped fresh
parsley

1 teaspoon sugar

125 g (4 oz) tiny button
mushrooms

12 fried bread croutons

fresh finely chopped parsley, to
garnish

Heat oil in a pan and gently fry veal in small batches for 3 to 4 minutes. Remove from pan, add extra oil if necessary, then fry onions until golden. Stir in the flour and cook until brown. Add the tomato paste, white wine and stock and heat, stirring until boiling.

Add the veal, garlic, bouquet garni and tomatoes, then season with salt and pepper, parsley and sugar. Cover the pan and simmer gently for 30 to 40 minutes. Add the mushrooms and continue cooking for 10 to 12 minutes, or until the meat is tender.

Serve hot, garnished with the croutons and parsley, accompanied by rice and a green vegetable.

SERVES 6

ZUCCHINI LASAGNE

6 to 8 zucchini (courgettes),
trimmed and sliced lengthways

extra grated Parmesan cheese

TOMATO SAUCE

1 tablespoon vegetable oil

1 onion, finely chopped

250 g (8 oz) button mushrooms,
sliced

½ red capsicum (pepper), cut into
1 cm (½ in) pieces

2 tablespoons chopped fresh basil,
or 2 teaspoons dried basil
leaves

440 g (14 oz) can tomato pieces,
drained and chopped

4 tablespoons tomato paste

1 teaspoon sugar

SPINACH LAYER

1 bunch English spinach or
silverbeet, washed, stalks
removed and chopped

1 clove garlic, finely chopped

1 onion, finely chopped

¼ teaspoon ground nutmeg

MORNAY SAUCE

¾ cup (185 ml/6 fl oz) milk

1 small onion, chopped

4 cloves

1 bay leaf

30 g (1 oz) butter

2 tablespoons plain flour

60 g (2 oz) grated tasty cheese

CHEESE LAYER

500 g (1 lb) ricotta cheese

60 g (2 oz) grated Parmesan
cheese

2 eggs, beaten

Preheat oven to 190°C (375°F).

To Prepare Tomato Sauce: Heat oil in a large pan and gently fry onion, mushrooms and capsicum until tender. Add basil, tomatoes, tomato paste and sugar. Simmer uncovered for 30 minutes, then set aside.

To Prepare Spinach Layer: Place spinach leaves, garlic, onion and nutmeg in a saucepan and cook covered for 3 to 5 minutes, or until the spinach has wilted. Drain well, squeezing the spinach to remove all excess liquid. Set aside.

To Prepare Mornay Sauce: Heat milk with the onion, cloves and bay leaf. Stand for 30 minutes then strain, discarding flavourings. Melt butter in a saucepan and add the flour. Cook for 1 minute, stirring continuously, or until foaming but not brown. Add the milk and cook, stirring until boiling. Fold in the cheese and remove from the heat. Cover closely with waxed paper or clear plastic until required.

To Prepare Cheese Layer: Combine ricotta and Parmesan cheeses with the eggs and reserve.

To Assemble: Pour half the Tomato Sauce into a greased casserole dish and top with a layer of zucchini. Top with the spinach mixture, remaining tomato sauce and cheese layer. Cover with the remaining zucchini. Pour the Mornay Sauce evenly over and sprinkle with extra Parmesan cheese. Bake in oven for 30 to 45 minutes or until the top is golden and bubbling.

Serve with warm Italian bread rolls.

SERVES 4 TO 6

CHILLI CON CARNE

Chilli Con Carne improves in flavour if made in advance. It freezes well and is suitable for a main course or for a buffet meal.

1 tablespoon oil

1 onion, sliced

500 g (1 lb) beef topside, finely
minced

1 green capsicum (pepper),
chopped

1 clove garlic, crushed

425 g (13½ oz) can tomato pieces

465 g (15 oz) can red kidney
beans

250 g (8 oz) can tomato paste

2 teaspoons chilli powder

1 teaspoon salt

1 tablespoon chopped fresh basil

Heat oil in a large pan, add onion, crumble in the mince and fry over high heat for 5 minutes, stirring occasionally. Pour off any excess fat, then stir in the remaining ingredients. Bring the mixture to the boil, cover and simmer for 1 hour, stirring occasionally. Serve with rice and sour cream or guacamole.

SERVES 6

LAMB AND YOGHURT CURRY

- 750 g (1½ lb) lean lamb
- ½ cup (125 ml/4 fl oz) natural yoghurt
- ½ teaspoon salt
- 30 g (1 oz) ghee or butter
- 3 onions, chopped
- 2 tablespoons garam masala
- ¼ teaspoon chilli powder
- 3 cloves garlic, crushed
- 375 g (12 oz) tomatoes, cored, peeled and chopped
- 1 cup (250 ml/8 fl oz) coconut milk

Cut lamb into 2.5 cm (1 in) cubes. Mix yoghurt and salt together in a non-metallic dish and add the lamb. Marinate for 30 minutes.

Heat ghee in a heavy-based pan and fry onions until soft, then add the garam masala and chilli powder. Cook for 2 minutes, stirring. Add the garlic, lamb (with marinade) and tomatoes, and bring to the boil. Stir in the coconut milk, cover pan and cook over a low heat for 1 hour or until the lamb is tender.

Serve Lamb and Yoghurt Curry with rice and curry accompaniments.

SERVES 6

STUFFED EGGPLANT (AUBERGINE)

- 2 medium eggplants (aubergines)
- 30 g (1 oz) butter or margarine
- 1 tablespoon plain flour
- ½ teaspoon ground nutmeg
- salt and pepper
- 1 cup (250 ml/8 fl oz) milk
- 1 tablespoon olive oil
- 2 onions, chopped
- 2 cloves garlic, crushed
- 2 tomatoes, cored and chopped
- 425 g (13½ oz) can soy beans
- 1 tablespoon chopped, fresh parsley
- 1 teaspoon chopped, fresh oregano
- 125 g (4 oz) grated cheddar cheese
- 30 g (1 oz) fresh breadcrumbs

Preheat oven to 180°C (350°F).

Slice eggplant (aubergine) in half lengthways, scoop out seeds and flesh, leaving a shell of 1 cm (½ in). Sprinkle well with salt and allow to stand 30 minutes. Chop reserved flesh.

Melt butter in saucepan and stir in flour, nutmeg, salt and pepper. Cook over medium heat for 1 minute, stirring continuously. Gradually add milk, stirring until sauce thickens and boils. Cool slightly, cover and set aside.

Heat oil and gently fry onions and garlic for 5 minutes. Add eggplant (aubergine) flesh, chopped tomatoes, soy beans, parsley and oregano and simmer for 15 minutes.

Rinse eggplant shells, pat dry and place in a baking dish. Spoon equal quantities of tomato mixture into each half. Top with white sauce. Combine grated cheese and breadcrumbs, and sprinkle on top. Bake until eggplant is soft but not split. If necessary, place under griller to brown top before serving.

Serve accompanied by lemon-flavoured rice.

SERVES 4

CRAB AND PRAWN (SHRIMP) CREOLE

- 1 tablespoon olive oil
- 20 g (⅔ oz) butter
- 1 small green capsicum (pepper), chopped
- 1 small onion, chopped
- 555 g (18 oz) cooked rice (220 g (7 oz) raw)
- ¾ cup (185 ml/6 fl oz) white wine
- 2 tomatoes, chopped
- salt
- cayenne pepper
- freshly ground black pepper
- dash Tabasco sauce
- 250 g (8 oz) fresh crabmeat
- 500 g (1 lb) prawns (shrimps), shelled and deveined
- lemon slices and parsley sprigs, to garnish

Heat oil and butter in a heavy-based pan and gently fry the capsicum and onion until soft but not browned. Stir in the rice, mixing until well coated with oil and butter.

Blend in the wine and tomatoes, and season with salt, cayenne, pepper and Tabasco sauce. Simmer over low heat, stirring constantly, for 5 to 10 minutes, or until the mixture has thickened slightly.

Fold crabmeat and prawns (shrimps) into creole rice and heat through gently.

To Serve: Spoon into a heated serving dish or into individual bowls and garnish with lemon and parsley. Serve with a tossed green salad.

SERVES 4

Right: Lamb Noisettes Italian Style

LAMB NOISETTES ITALIAN STYLE

1 boned, rolled loin of lamb
  or 6 lamb noisettes

salt and pepper

olive oil

SAUCE

3 tablespoons grated Parmesan
  cheese

3 tablespoons chopped fresh
  parsley

salt and pepper

2 cloves garlic, finely chopped

1 cup Napoletana Sauce (see
  recipe page 15)

1 tablespoon chopped fresh basil

arugula (rocket) or watercress
  sprigs, to garnish

Ask your butcher to cut the loin of lamb into 6 thick slices or noisettes. Secure the noisettes in neat rounds with skewers or wooden toothpicks.

Season the lamb with salt and pepper, then brush with oil. Place on a greased, foil-lined baking tray and grill quickly for 2 minutes on each side under a hot grill to seal the meat.

To Prepare Sauce: Combine all the sauce ingredients.

Baste the noisettes with the sauce and continue cooking on a lower heat for 7 to 8 minutes on both sides. Baste the lamb several times during cooking.

Serve garnished with sprigs of arugula, accompanied by rice and green salad.

SERVES 6

SPICY TOMATO SCALLOPS

1 tablespoon olive oil

2 cloves garlic, crushed

2 white onions, finely chopped

250 g (8 oz) scallops, deveined

2 tablespoons chopped parsley

1 teaspoon chopped ginger

1 teaspoon minced chillies

salt and pepper

2 tablespoons tomato paste

2 tablespoons fresh breadcrumbs

1 tablespoon olive oil, extra

lemon, to garnish

Preheat oven to 220°C (425°F).

Heat oil in a frying pan, add garlic and onions and cook over low heat for 3 minutes, or until tender.

Add scallops, parsley, ginger, chillies, salt, pepper and tomato paste. Spoon the mixture into 4 scallop shells or individual shallow ovenproof dishes. Sprinkle the breadcrumbs and olive oil over the top. Bake in an oven for 15 to 20 minutes, or until lightly browned. Serve garnished with lemon twists or wedges.

SERVES 4 AS AN ENTREE

Sun-dried Tomatoes, Chutneys and Preserves

*O*ne of the best things to do with tomatoes is to preserve those you cannot use — there are usually too many at their peak of ripeness simultaneously during the local season. Oven 'sun-drying' and making chutneys, sauces, pickles and relishes are all popular possibilities. Preserved tomatoes are good for fêtes, as gifts and, of course, can be used in your own menus at home.

HOME-MADE TOMATO SAUCE

2 kg (4 lb) tomatoes, cored and chopped

2 cups (500 ml/16 fl oz) vinegar

500 g (1 lb) sugar

4 tablespoons salt

1 teaspoon cayenne pepper

4 tablespoons black peppercorns

4 tablespoons whole allspice

4 tablespoons crushed cinnamon sticks

2 tablespoons mustard seeds

2 tablespoons cloves

Put the tomatoes in a pan and cook gently until reduced to a pulp. Rub through a colander to remove the skin and seeds.

Return the strained pulp to the pan and cook with the vinegar and sugar gently for 2 hours or until thick, then season with salt and cayenne pepper. Tie the spices in a piece of muslin cloth and drop into the mixture. Gently boil, stirring occasionally, until the sauce reaches the desired consistency. Remove spices. Bottle and seal while hot.

Store in a cool, dark pantry or cupboard. Serve with home-made chips!

TOMATO PUREE

12 large, ripe tomatoes

1 cup diced green capsicum (pepper)

4 large onions, chopped

1 stick celery, sliced

4 tablespoons sugar

1 tablespoon salt

Core the tomatoes and cut them into thin wedges. Place all the ingredients in a pan, bring to a simmer over medium heat then cover and simmer for 35 to 40 minutes until the tomatoes have broken down to a pulp.

Spoon the mixture into an electric blender or food processor and process until smooth. This may be done in several batches. Pour the purée through a sieve and back into the rinsed-out pan and bring to the boil. Cook at a full rolling boil for 30 minutes, stirring occasionally.

Pour into hot, sterilised jars leaving a little space at the top of each jar. Screw the tops on the jars tightly. Bring a large pan of water to the boil. Carefully lower the filled jars into the pan and cook in the boiling water for 30 minutes. Lift from the pan and allow the jars to cool. Store in a cool, dark cupboard for up to 6 months. Refrigerate after opening.

MAKES 3 LITRES (5 PINTS)

TOMATO FLAVOURED OIL

Use this in place of French Dressing for salads.

1.5 kg (3 lb) tomatoes

½ cup (125 ml/4 fl oz) olive oil

1 tablespoon chopped, fresh tarragon

salt

freshly ground black pepper

Blanch tomatoes, remove skin. Cut tomatoes in half and squeeze out seeds. Remove cores. Mix tomato flesh to a purée in a food processor or blender.

Place purée in a saucepan and boil on medium heat for 30 minutes to reduce. Strain purée and leave to cool.

Mix oil, tarragon and salt and pepper with the tomato purée. Pour into a glass jar, cover and store in refrigerator.

Use as required for dressing salads.

NON-REACTIVE PANS

- When cooking with tomato it is best to use a non-reactive pan.

- A non-reactive pan can be stainless steel, enamel or heat proof glass, but not aluminium.

- Use of an non-reactive pan ensures that the flavours don't "react" with the pan. Such reaction can cause bitterness and discolouration of the food.

Pictured on previous pages: Oven Sun-dried Tomatoes in Oil, Oven Dried Tomatoes (page 88)

FRUITY TOMATO CHUTNEY

Mix tomatoes with the fruits of summer, and enjoy them in this all-year-round chutney.

>   1.5 kg (3 lb) apples, peeled, cored and chopped
>
>   1.5 kg (3 lb) tomatoes, peeled, cored and chopped
>
>   250 g (8 oz) garlic, chopped
>
>   1 kg (2 lb) plums, stoned
>
>   1.5 kg (3 lb) marrow, seeded and chopped
>
>   1 kg (2¼ lb) onions, chopped
>
>   250 g (8 oz) French shallots, chopped
>
>   1 kg (2 lb) sugar
>
>   6 tablespoons salt
>
>   6 tablespoons mustard seed
>
>   1 tablespoon chopped ginger
>
>   1 teaspoon chopped red chillies
>
>   1 teaspoon cloves

Simmer the apples in just enough water to cover until tender. Transfer to a large bowl and add the tomatoes, garlic, plums, vegetables, sugar and salt. Leave to stand overnight.

The next day, tie the spices in a piece of muslin cloth and add this spice bag to the vegetable mixture. Simmer for 4 hours, or until the chutney reaches the desired consistency.

Pour chutney into warm jars and seal while hot. Store in a cool, dry, dark cupboard.

CHILLIES

Take care when cutting chillies. Their juices are very strong and can burn skin and eyes. Use rubber gloves when cutting chillies to avoid burns.

TOMATO CHUTNEY

>   12 large ripe tomatoes, cored, peeled and chopped
>
>   6 medium apples, peeled, cored and chopped
>
>   6 red capsicums (peppers), seeded and chopped
>
>   4 green capsicums (peppers), seeded and chopped
>
>   4 large onions, chopped
>
>   1 red chilli, seeded and chopped
>
>   250 g (8 oz) seedless raisins
>
>   1 cup (250 ml/8 fl oz) white vinegar
>
>   1 tablespoon brown sugar
>
>   2 teaspoons celery seeds
>
>   1 teaspoon salt

Mix all the ingredients together in a large pan and bring to the boil. Cook on a low heat for 1 hour, stirring occasionally, until the chutney reaches the desired consistency. Bottle and seal while hot. Store in a dry, cool, dark cupboard.

GREEN TOMATO AND APPLE CHUTNEY

>   12 black peppercorns
>
>   small knob ginger, bruised
>
>   1 tablsespoon dried red chillies
>
>   8 cups (2 litres/70 fl oz) vinegar
>
>   500 g (1 lb) sugar
>
>   4 tablespoons salt
>
>   2 kg (4 lb) green tomatoes, finely chopped
>
>   500 g (1 lb) marrow, seeded and finely chopped
>
>   500 g (1 lb) French shallots, finely chopped
>
>   1.5 kg apples, peeled, cored and finely chopped
>
>   500 g (1 lb) sultanas
>
>   juice of 3 lemons

Tie the spices into a piece of muslin cloth and add them to the vinegar, sugar and salt. Boil gently for 50 minutes, stirring occasionally. Add the vegetables and fruit to the vinegar with the lemon juice, bring to the boil and simmer for 3½ to 4 hours, or until the chutney reaches the desired consistency. If necessary, add more vinegar. Bottle and seal while hot. Store in a dry, cool, dark cupboard.

OVEN-DRIED TOMATOES

Pictured on pages 84-85.

A simple way to preserve ripe tomatoes when you have a glut of home-grown tomatoes.

Preheat oven to 100°C (200°F).

Slice tomatoes in half through the stalk or calyx. Scoop out the seeds with a metal teaspoon.

Line the bottom of the oven with aluminium foil. Place the tomatoes, cut side down, on the oven racks. Leave to dry out for 12 hours. If using a fan-forced oven, leave for 6 to 8 hours until dry.

Store oven-dried tomatoes in a glass jar when cold.

OVEN 'SUN-DRIED' TOMATOES IN OIL

Pictured on pages 84-85.

Make these when tomatoes are in season. Use locally grown vine-ripened tomatoes if possible — they have the best flavour. Italian plum or standard varieties are all suitable.

> *2 kg (4 lb) ripe tomatoes*
> *2 tablespoons olive oil*
> *2 teaspoons crushed garlic*
> *freshly ground black pepper*
> *extra olive oil*

Preheat oven to 100°C (200°F).

Core tomatoes with a sharp pointed knife, then cut in half from top to bottom and squeeze out the seeds or scoop them out with a teaspoon. Place cut side down on an oiled, foil-lined baking tray. Mix olive oil with garlic and brush over tomatoes, then sprinkle them with pepper.

Place in oven for 6 hours.

Place tomatoes in clean warm jars, cover with olive oil, seal and chill quickly in refrigerator until cold. Store in a cool, dry, dark cupboard.

Use sun-dried tomatoes in salads, pasta sauces and antipasto.

Remove core from tomatoes, cut in half lengthwise and squeeze out seeds.

Place tomatoes cut side down on an oiled foil-lined baking tray, brush with olive oil and crushed garlic and season with freshly ground black pepper.

Bake tomatoes for six hours, then place dried tomatoes in clean jars and cover with olive oil.

Tomato Rose

With a small sharp knife, cut a slice from the base of a firm tomato and continue peeling the fruit in a spiral, taking care not to break the skin. Place the peel on a board and loosely wind it to form a neat roll like the base of a rose and secure with a toothpick. Wind a second piece of skin tightly to form the rose's centre, place it in the middle and secure with a toothpick.

Tomato Tulip

Making six diagonal cuts, slice halfway down the tomato and peel the skin back with a small sharp knife, taking care not to cut it too finely as the peel will dry out. The tomato tulip provides an attractive garnish for salads, seafood platters and glazed legs of ham.

Vandycking Tomatoes

Using a sharp knife, cut through the centre of the tomato in a zigzag fashion and carefully divide in two when the fruit has been cut all the way round.

PEELING TOMATOES

The wide availability of ready-peeled, low cost canned tomatoes makes this an unnecessary exercise when preparing a simple casserole or soup, but there are some recipes for which freshly peeled tomatoes are invaluable.

To peel ripe fruit, use a small, sharp knife to score the circumference of the tomatoes with a cross.

Put the tomatoes in a bowl and pour boiling water over them, leaving them to soak for 10 seconds or until the skin starts peeling back.

Remove and place in a bowl of cold water. Drain tomatoes one by one and strip the skin off, then cut out the calyx or core at the stem end with a sharp-pointed knife.

SEEDING TOMATOES

It is very simple to remove the seeds from tomatoes and the little time and effort it takes will be amply rewarded in your cooking.

The little seeds in tomatoes can spoil the appearance and texture of some recipes and, when cooked, may impart a slightly bitter taste to a delicately flavoured dish.

All you do is cut the tomato in half, crosswise, and gently squeeze each half over a sieve. Scoop out any remaining seeds with a teaspoon.

Discard the seeds and reserve the liquid to use in your cooking, in a soup or casserole.

MAKING TOMATO CONCENTRATE

Peeled and seeded tomatoes can be cooked into a versatile pulp which can be sieved to make a soup or sauce, added to thicken a casserole or gently reduced to a thick concentrate.

Concentrated tomato paste is the best way to freeze tomatoes as it takes up minimum space and you can reuse it by diluting it with stock, water or wine to the desired consistency.

The pulp or concentrate can be frozen in small containers or ice cube trays and then removed and stored in a plastic bag.

The pulp will keep for a year unless the tomatoes were very ripe when cooked. In this case it is best to keep the pulp frozen for no more than one month.

STERILISING JARS

To sterilise jars, first wash them in hot, soapy water. Rinse with boiling water then turn the jars upside down on a clean dry tea towel. Using tongs, place the jars on a baking tray.

Place in the oven at 150°C (300°F) for 15 minutes. The jars are now ready to be filled with hot preserves.

GREEN TOMATO PICKLE

Wait until the frosts have taken the vines, and then use the remaining crop of green tomatoes for this pickle.

3 kg (6 lb) green tomatoes, cored and sliced

1 kg (2 lb) onions, sliced

6 tablespoons salt

2 cups (500 ml/16 fl oz) white vinegar

375 g (12 oz) sugar

3 whole cloves

1 tablespoon ground mustard

2 teaspoons cornflour

Layer the tomatoes alternately with the onions in a glass bowl, lightly sprinkling each layer with salt. Leave to stand overnight.

The next day, bring the vinegar, sugar and cloves to the boil in a large pan. Make a paste of the mustard and cornflour and stir in a little vinegar to blend. Stir into the boiling vinegar. Rinse and drain the tomatoes and onions and add to the vinegar. Bring to the boil and cook for 1 hour, stirring occasionally, until the pickle reaches the desired consistency. Bottle and seal while hot. Store in a dry, cool, dark cupboard.

TOMATO AND CUCUMBER PICKLE

3 kg (6 lb) green tomatoes, cored and sliced

1 kg (2 lb) cucumbers, peeled and thinly sliced

220 g (7 oz) salt

2 red capsicums (peppers), seeded and finely chopped

3 cloves garlic, finely chopped

4 cups (1 litre/32 fl oz) white vinegar

375 g (12 oz) sugar

1 tablespoon ground mustard

2 teaspoons ground turmeric

1 teaspoon ground allspice

1 teaspoon celery salt

Mix the tomatoes and cucumbers in a bowl, sprinkle evenly with salt and leave overnight.

The next day, rinse and drain the tomato and cucumber mixture then combine with the remaining ingredients in a large pan. Bring to the boil, cook gently for 1 hour, stirring occasionally, until the pickle reaches the desired consistency.

Pour into hot sterilised jars and seal. Store in a cool, dark cupboard for up to 1 year. Refrigerate after opening.

TOMATO RELISH

3 kg (6 lb) tomatoes, cored, peeled and chopped

1 kg (2 lb) white onions, finely chopped

6 tablespoons salt

2 cups (500 ml/16 fl oz) vinegar

375 g (12 oz) sugar

2 tablespoons curry powder

1 tablespoon ground mustard

1 teaspoon ground mace

1 teaspoon ground cloves

1 teaspoon ground cinnamon

1 teaspoon ground ginger

1 teaspoon ground nutmeg

3 tablespoons cornflour

Mix the tomatoes and onions in a bowl, sprinkle with the salt and leave overnight.

The next day, rinse and drain the tomato mixture. Place in a large pan, cover with the vinegar, then add the sugar. Bring to the boil and simmer, stirring constantly, until the sugar has dissolved. Mix the spices with the cornflour and blend with a little cold vinegar. Pour the paste into the relish and cook gently for 1 hour, stirring occasionally, until the relish is the desired consistency.

Bottle and seal while hot. Store in a dry, cool, dark cupboard.

Testing jam for setting point (Method 1) Remove a small amount of hot jam with a spoon. Tilt the spoon, and if the jam comes away in large flake-like drops — not too runny — it has reached setting point.

Testing jam for setting point (Method 2) Spoon some hot jam onto a chilled saucer. Allow to cool, then gently push your finger into the jam. If it wrinkles on top the jam is at setting point.

PINEAPPLE AND TOMATO JAM

1 large pineapple

1 kg (2 lb) tomatoes, cored and peeled

375 g (12 oz) sugar for each 500 g (1 lb) pineapple and tomato purée (see method)

Cut the pineapple in half and cut out the flesh. Place flesh in a large pan with the tomatoes. Bring slowly to a simmer and cook until the pineapple is soft. Carefully weigh the mixture and return to the saucepan. Add the sugar according to weight. Return to heat and simmer, stirring until the sugar dissolves.

Bring to the boil and skim off any impurities that rise to the top. Boil for 1 hour, or until the jam forms thick droplets when dropped from a metal spoon. Pour the jam into hot, sterilised jars and seal with tight-fitting lids.

PRESERVES AS GIFTS

Homemade chutneys, relishes, sun-dried tomatoes and flavoured oils make wonderful gifts. Collect interesting shaped jars for the purpose. Remember to sterilize and warm the jars before pouring in the preserves and allow filled jars to cool before sealing. As a final decorative touch cut circles out of checked or floral fabric (or paper), large enough to cover the lids generously. Tie raffia or rustic string around the tops of the jars, securing the circles of fabric in place. Remember to put sticky labels on the fronts of the jars stating what they contain!

HINTS FOR JAM MAKING

To prevent fruit catching and burning on the bottom of the pan, rub a little butter inside the base of the pan before using it.

If you have a sugar thermometer, jam will reach 105°C (221°F) when it has reached its setting point.

To sterilise jars, first wash them in hot, soapy water. Rinse with boiling water then turn the jars upside down on a clean dry tea towel. Using tongs, place the jars on a baking tray. Place in the oven at 150°C (300°F) for 15 minutes. The jars are now ready to be filled with hot preserves.

TOMATO MARMALADE

4 oranges

1 lemon

2 kg (4 lb) tomatoes, cored, peeled and chopped

2 kg (4 lb) sugar

Finely slice the oranges and lemon, leaving the rind on. Add to the tomatoes and sugar in a large pan and bring to the boil, stirring occasionally. Reduce the heat and cook gently for 1 hour, or until the mixture forms thick droplets when dropped from a metal spoon. Pour into hot, sterilised jars and seal with tight-fitting lids. This marmalade can be stored for up to 2 years.

Tomato Preserves

Measuring Made Easy

How to Measure Liquids

METRIC	IMPERIAL	CUPS
30 ml	1 fl oz	1 tablespoon plus 2 teaspoons
60 ml	2 fl oz	¼ cup
90 ml	3 fl oz	
125 ml	4 fl oz	½ cup
150 ml	5 fl oz	
170 ml	5½ fl oz	
180 ml	6 fl oz	¾ cup
220 ml	7 fl oz	
250 ml	8 fl oz	1 cup
500 ml	16 fl oz	2 cups
600 ml	20 fl oz (1 pint)	2½ cups

How to Measure Dry Ingredients

15 g	½ oz	
30 g	1 oz	
60 g	2 oz	
90 g	3 oz	
125 g	4 oz	(¼ lb)
155 g	5 oz	
185 g	6 oz	
220 g	7 oz	
250 g	8 oz	(½ lb)
280 g	9 oz	
315 g	10 oz	
345 g	11 oz	
375 g	12 oz	(¾ lb)
410 g	13 oz	
440 g	14 oz	
470 g	15 oz	
500 g	16 oz	(1 lb)
750 g	24 oz	(1½ lb)
1 kg	32 oz	(2 lb)

Quick Conversions

5 mm	¼ in	
1 cm	½ in	
2 cm	¾ in	
2.5 cm	1 in	
5 cm	2 in	
6 cm	2½ in	
8 cm	3 in	
10 cm	4 in	
12 cm	5 in	
15 cm	6 in	
18 cm	7 in	
20 cm	8 in	
23 cm	9 in	
25 cm	10 in	
28 cm	11 in	
30 cm	12 in	(1 ft)
46 cm	18 in	
50 cm	20 in	
61 cm	24 in	(2 ft)

Note:

We developed the recipes in this book in Australia where the tablespoon measure is 20 ml. In many other countries the tablespoon is 15 ml. For most recipes this difference will not be noticeable. However, for recipes using baking powder, gelatine, bicarbonate of soda, small amounts of flour and cornflour, we suggest you add an extra teaspoon for each tablespoon specified.

Using Cups and Spoons

All cup and spoon measurements are level

METRIC CUP				METRIC SPOONS	
¼ cup	60 ml	2 fl oz		¼ teaspoon	1.25 ml
⅓ cup	80 ml	2½ fl oz		½ teaspoon	2.5 ml
½ cup	125 ml	4 fl oz		1 teaspoon	5 ml
1 cup	250 ml	8 fl oz		1 tablespoon	20 ml

Oven Temperatures

TEMPERATURES	CELSIUS (°C)	FAHRENHEIT (°F)	GAS MARK
Very slow	120	250	½
Slow	150	300	2
Moderately slow	160-180	325-350	3-4
Moderate	190-200	375-400	5-6
Moderately hot	220-230	425-450	7
Hot	250-260	475-500	8-9

Index

Anchovy and tomato flan 43
Apple and green tomato
  chutney 87
Artichoke, tomato and
  anchovy pizzas 32
Aubergine see Eggplant
Avocado
  and tomato focaccia 68
  and tomato shells 48

Baked fish Spanish style 80
Barbecue sauce 15
Barbecued pork spare ribs 79
Basil
  butter 64
  and cherry tomato
    salad 48
  pesto dressing 55
Beans with Provençale
  sauce 19
Beef chilli con carne 81
Beverages see Coolers; Juice
Bloody Mary 58
Blue cheese and onion
  quiches 41
Bocconcini and tomato
  salad 52
Butter, basil 64

Calamari and oyster fritters
  with tomato seafood
  sauce 15
Capsicum see Red pepper
Cauliflower
  koftas in hot tomato
    sauce 14
  and tomato gratin 70
Cheese
  and onion quiches 41
  soufflé in tomatoes 70
  and tomato quiche 43
  and tomato quiche
    Lorraine 38
Cherry tomatoes
  and basil salad 48
  hummus-stuffed 63
Chick peas
  hummus-stuffed cherry
    tomatoes 63
  and tomato subji 17
Chicken
  cacciatore 77
  chasseur 79

and tomato croissants 71
Chicken liver snack 64
Chilled soup
  gazpacho 29
  no-cook tomato 29
  tomato dill 29
Chilli con carne 81
Chutney
  fruity tomato 87
  green tomato and
    apple 87
  tomato 87
  tomato relish 91
Citrus
  and tomato marmalade 92
  tomato salad 57
Consommé, tomato 26
Coolers
  see also Juice
  tomato refresher 58
  yoghurt tomato mix 58
  zesty Bloody Mary 58
Coulis, tomato, with
  crumbed sardines 20
Courgette lasagne 81
Crab and prawn Creole 82
Crayfish with tomato and
  wine 74
Creole sauce 80
Croissants, chicken and
  tomato 71
Crostini, sun-dried tomato
  pâté 68
Crudités with Thai tomato
  dip 68
Cucumber and tomato
  pickle 91
Curry
  lamb and yoghurt 82
  tomato sauce with
    prawns 19

Dip
  Thai tomato, with
    crudités 68
  yoghurt tomato, with
    pakoras 62
Dressing
  French 57
  pesto 55
  tomato flavoured oil 86
Dried tomatoes see Oven-
  dried tomatoes; Sun-dried
  tomatoes
Drinks see Coolers; Juice

Eggplant
  ratatouille 54
  stuffed 82
  and tomato pie 43

Farmhouse salad 55
Fennel and tomato soup 28
Filo pie, tomato and
  carrot 32
Fish
  see also Sardines
  baked Spanish style 80
  smoked, and tomato
    soup 25
  tomato and anchovy
    flan 43
  tomatoes and salmon on
    rye 62
Fisherman's basket with wine
  tomato salsa 16
Flan see Tart
Focaccia, tomato and
  avocado 68
French dressing 57
Fried green tomatoes 67
Fritters, oyster and calamari,
  with tomato seafood
  sauce 15
Fruity tomato chutney 87

Gazpacho 29
Gnocchi with ripe tomato
  sauce 12
Greek salad 55
Green beans with Provençale
  sauce 19
Green tomatoes
  and apple chutney 87
  fried 67
  pickle 91
Grilled tomato and red
  pepper soup 28
Gruyère and tomato
  quiche 43

Herbed tomato juice 59
Hot tomato salsa 16
Hot turkey and tomato
  melts 62
Hummus-stuffed cherry
  tomatoes 63

Italian eggplant and tomato
  pie 43
Italian noodle soup 25
Italian stuffed mussels 74

Jam
  pineapple and tomato 92
  tomato marmalade 92
Juice
  herbed 59
  minted 59
  sherried 59

Koftas, cauliflower, in hot
  tomato sauce 14

Lamb
  noisettes Italian style 83
  and yoghurt curry 82
Lasagne
  easy 79
  zucchini 81

Marmalade, tomato 92
Melts, hot turkey and
  tomato 62
Middle-Eastern tomatoes 71
Minestrone 24
Minted tomato juice 59
Mixed tomato tart 37
Mornay sauce 81
Mushroom and tomato pasta
  sauce 14
Mussels, Italian stuffed 74

Napolitana sauce 15
No-cook tomato soup 29
Noodle soup, Italian 25

Oil, tomato flavoured 86
Old-fashioned tomato
  soup 24
Olive and tomato pasta
  sauce 20
Omelette
  red pepper and
    tomato 67
  tomato 67
Onion
  and blue cheese
    quiches 41
  and tomato salad 57
  and tomato tart
    Niçoise 38
Open sandwiches 65
  tomatoes and salmon on
    rye 62
Orange and creamy tomato
  soup 29
Oven-dried tomatoes 88
  in oil 88

Oyster and calamari fritters with tomato seafood sauce 15
Pakoras with yoghurt tomato dip 62
Pasta salad with pesto dressing 55
Pasta sauce
  Napolitana 15
  ripe tomato 12
  sun-dried tomato pesto 12
  tomato and mushroom 14
  tomato and olive 20
Pâté, sun-dried tomato, with crostini 68
Penne with tomato and olive sauce 20
Pepper, red see Red pepper
Pesto
  dressing 55
  sun-dried tomato 12
Pickle
  see also Chutney
  green tomato 91
  tomato and cucumber 91
Pie
  see also Tart
  Italian eggplant and tomato 43
  piperade 38
  tomato and carrot filo 32
Pikelets, sun-dried tomato 63
Pilaf, rice and tomato 70
Pineapple and tomato jam 92
Piperade pie 38
Pissaladière 42
Pizza
  wholemeal dough 32
  marinara 35
  Napolitana 37
  tomato, artichoke and anchovy 32
  tomato and fresh sardine 35
  vegetarian 35
Pork spare ribs, barbecued 79
Potage pistou 25
Prawns
  and crab Creole 82
  with curried tomato sauce 19

Provençale sauce with green beans 19
Pumpkin and tomato soup 24
Purée, tomato 86

Quiche
  cheese and tomato 38
  onion and blue cheese 41
  tomato and Gruyère 43

Ratatouille 54
Red pepper
  and grilled tomato soup 28
  and tomato omelette 67
Relish see Chutney
Rice and tomato pilaf 70
Ricotta and tomato salad 54

Salad
  bocconcini and tomato 52
  cherry tomato and basil 48
  farmhouse 55
  Greek 55
  Niçoise 54
  pasta, with pesto dressing 55
  ricotta and tomato 54
  tomato and onion 57
  tomato and yoghurt 48
  tomato citrus 57
  tomatoes vinaigrette 56
Salmon and tomatoes on rye 62
Salsa
  fresh tomato 16
  hot tomato, with stuffed squid 16
  wine tomato 16
Sandwiches, open see Open sandwiches
Sardines
  crumbed, with tomato coulis 20
  and tomato pizza 35
Sauce
  see also Pasta sauce; Salsa
  Creole 80
  curried tomato, with prawns 19
  home-made tomato 86

hot tomato 14
Napolitana 15
Provençal, with green beans 19
sweet and sour tomato 17
tasty tomato 19
tomato barbecue 15
tomato coulis 20
tomato seafood 15
Savoury tomato cases 63
Scallops, spicy tomato 83
Seafood
  curried tomato sauce with prawns 19
  fisherman's basket with wine tomato salsa 16
  Italian stuffed mussels 74
  pizza marinara 35
  spicy tomato scallops 83
  and tomato sauce with oyster and calamari fritters 15
Sherried tomato juice 59
Shrimps see Prawns
Smoked fish and tomato soup 25
Soufflé, cheese, with tomatoes 70
Soup
  see also Chilled soup
  grilled tomato and red pepper 28
  Italian noodle 25
  minestrone 24
  old-fashioned tomato 24
  orange and creamy tomato 29
  potage pistou 25
  tomato and pumpkin 24
  tomato and smoked fish 25
  tomato and vegetable 28
  tomato consommé 26
  tomato fennel 28
Spare ribs, barbecued 79
Speedy pizza Napolitana 37
Spicy tomato scallops 83
Spinach-stuffed tomatoes 71
Squid, stuffed, with hot tomato salsa 16
Stuffed eggplant 82
Stuffed tomatoes

avocado shells 48
with hummus 63
Middle Eastern 71
with spinach 71
Subji, tomato and chick pea 17
Sun-dried tomatoes
  pâté crostini 68
  pesto 12
  pikelets 63
Sweet and sour tomato sauce with vegetables 17

Tart
  see also Quiche
  mixed tomato 37
  piperade pie 38
  pissaladière 42
  tomato and anchovy 43
  tomato and onion 38
Tasty tomato sauce 19
Thai tomato dip with crudités 68
Tofu with peas and tomatoes 17
Turkey and tomato melts 62

Veal
  Marengo 80
  Parmigiana 76
Vegetables
  crudités with Thai tomato dip 68
  pizza 35
  with sweet and sour tomato sauce 17
  and tomato soup 28
Vegetarian pizza 35
Vinaigrette tomatoes 56
Vol-au-vents, savoury tomato 63

Wholemeal pizza dough 32
Wine tomato salsa 16

Yoghurt
  tomato dip with pakoras 62
  tomato mix 58
  and tomato salad 48

Zesty Bloody Mary 58
Zucchini lasagne 81